MIDGE

JON WALLER

MIDGE

A STORY OF A FEARLESS, STRONG WOMAN AND HER LINEAGE

Kravitz & Sons
INNOVATORS IN PUBLISHING, MARKETING AND ADVERTISING

Kravitz and Sons LLC
1301 Farmville Blvd, Suite 104
Greenville, NC 27834

Published by Kravitz and Sons LLC.

ISBN: 979-8-89639-168-5 (sc)
ISBN: 979-8-89639-167-8 (e)

Library of Congress Control Number: 2025907475

Because of the dynamic nature of the Internet, any web addresses or links contained in this book may have changed since publication and may no longer be valid. The views expressed in this work are solely those of the author and do not necessarily reflect the views of the publisher, and the publisher hereby disclaims any responsibility for them.

TABLE OF CONTENTS

GRAND MOM

My hand reached up to grasp my Grand Mom's hand
She gently drew my hand into hers.
A calmness came over me as she walked along side me.
Slowing me down from my normal hurried pace,
She pointed out the wonders of the world I would have missed.
She patted my arm and all my fears seemed to fade away.
When I would say goodbye after a visit with her,
I would see the tears in her eyes.

Her touch was as gentle as the wing of a butterfly,
But tight as needed to warn of danger ahead.
No momma bear could have been more protective.
I was safeguarded from falls and bumps in the path.

She always knew what challenges were on the road before us.
I knew she loved me and her tender touch of her hand
Was proof of that immeasurable love.
How do I know this? I saw it every time she took my Grandfather's hand
And looked into his eyes when she thought I was not looking.

That same look was in her eyes as she watched over me.
Her advice, delivered in a matter of fact way, I would recall every day
of my life.

She seemed to know more each year or maybe her advice became wiser with time.
She could see the best in me when others could not.
Her encouragement was always sincere.
She always chose the right words that soothed my disappointments.

As we grew older, the time I spent with her would diminish;
But never the love.
She never forgot my birthdays, my anniversaries or my children's events.
She was always there to listen to my troubles and tell me hers.
While the years slowed her pace, she always knew the direction to go.

Now I hold her hand to steady her way.
I watch out for the dangers in the road ahead and give her advice.
I can comfort her with a pat of my hand on her arm.
Each visit brings us closer to the end and her goodbye brings tears to my eyes.
I hold her hand one last time as she held mine.
We both know the love that is there.

PROLOGUE

Our story dates back to the beginning of the Civil War and the era of the domination of the Great Plains by the American Indian through the settlement by fur trappers, traders and homesteaders to the end of the 19th Century, the Great War, the enfranchisement of women, the Roaring 20's, the Depression and the European theater of the Second World War. Through each of these eras, the women of our story play a part, along with the men in their lives, to overcome the hardships and twists of life that happen to them. Each of these events shape the landscape of our Country and particularly the upper Midwest. It was through the initiatives of the women, like those of this story that led to the expansion of the State of South Dakota, the securing of civil liberties for women throughout our country. It was the service of men like those in this story who sacrificed and served their country abroad and at home and how they inspired later generations of their family to even greater service to America. Finally, this is a story of love, a mother's love, a grandmother's love and indeed a great grandmother's love of their family. It is also the love of men for their spouses and country and finding love long after a search seems to have been lost.

CHAPTER 1

ANNA

Anna Brazos Marshall sat on the step of her sod hut behind her daughter's home outside of Bonesteel, South Dakota and stared at the sky. It was one of those evenings that was darkening at one edge of the sky and brightening at the other edge. The setting of the sun was occurring at the same time that the moon was beginning to rise. The air was crisp and a mist was covering the range, hovering above the creeks that cut across the farm. The cool breeze seemed to make the mist dance before it, separating the mist into ghost like figures. The higher the moon rose in the east, the brighter it became dividing the sky between darkness and light. She thought that the night was much like her, divided between the half of her that was white and the rest which was the white man referred to as Sioux. Anna knew that the whites had it wrong; the name was not Sioux but "Lakota". She always knew herself as Lakota rather than white. Balanced between white and Lakota, she found herself speaking the white man's language but thinking in Lakota. She knew the Christian God and their Savior Jesus but revered the Maka, the earth spirit and lover of the creator spirit Inyan. There were many gods in her Lakota world. The sacredness of life was in all things and even when she had ceased to follow the Lakota ways, she always respected the sacredness of every living thing. She looked at the full moon and knew that this full moon in October was called the harvest moon by the whites but for her it would always be the "Canwape Kasna Wi", meaning the moon of the "Wind that Shakes the Leaves". Despite the calmness of the night, she knew that this October night would lead, in a few weeks, to those winds that would shake the leaves from the trees. She did not need an almanac or a paper to know this. She just did.

Anna sat on the step and took out her pipe that she had smoked since she was a young woman. She often thought of her mother, her Ina who had been a full blooded Lakota. Her father had been a fur trapper and was French, one of the early ones that had come up the rivers to this part of the plains. It was an accepted custom for the early white adventurers to take an Indian as a spouse, although few made the arrangement permanent. Anna's parents did.

Anna was a beauty. Her hair was black and plentiful and the tone of her skin was copper but she had the cheekbones of her French forebears and the same full lips. Though short by today's standards, she was tall for a young Lakota. She learned to ride as well as she could run and her skills rivaled any full blooded Lakota. As a fur trapper's daughter she spent her youth learning, not only the ways of preparing furs, preserving the pelts, tanning hides into clothing and turning the flesh of the animals into edible food, but how to hunt and trap. Her Ina taught her the Lakota ways of preparing meals when the pots and kettles of the white man were not available. Fish and game would be wrapped in clay or mud and placed in the fire pit where it would cook in its own juices. When it was done, the clay would hardened and could be broken open exposing the fish or meat to be eaten once cool. Even birds could be cooked in this way with the feathers intact. Opening the hardened clay would strip the feathers from the flesh and the succulent meal could be eaten. There were no cook books to read. It was all handed down, mother to daughter and sometimes to son. These were necessary skills to have which would make the possessor a more suitable marriage prospect. Anna was a desirable young woman when she became of age. Unlike the female Lakota relatives that she had whose parents would select the proper suitor for their daughters, Anna had a strong streak of independence. She would decide to whom she would give herself. Whether it was the way she was brought up by her Ina, or just the way that she was, she knew that no one would ever make the decisions for her or anyone she would ever raise.

Anna could not remember when she first began to smoke. She had watched the trappers and the Lakota that hung around them do it and asked her father how to make a pipe. He was handy with a blade and taught her how to fashion one using handy tools and fire to hollow the stem and bowl of the pipe. Plants and spice and even tobacco would be the source of the fragrant smoke that would sometimes be inhaled. It was smoking her pipe squatting in front of her lodge that she saw a dark haired white man who had ridden to the outpost with furs. He was tall and lean with a full beard wearing a leather skin shirt and leggings. Though he was young, his beard hid that from those that met him. He rode bareback with the ease of any Lakota Anna had ever seen. When he spoke his voice literally boomed across the camp. He was from a place he called "Kentucky". He spoke French and a dialect of some of the more southern Native American tribes but one that she could understand. This man told her parents he was Charles Marshall and that he had furs to trade and needed to eat and spend the night. Her parents asked Charles to stay. Anna thought, as he entered their tipi, that he would do, yes, "this is the one". Anna was so smitten with Charles Marshall that she told her parents that night that she would wed him if he would have her. It was 1860 and the last year before the war between the states. Anna was barely 17 and Charles only 27. He would tell his children, many years later, he was swept off his feet by this beautiful Lakota woman; she was like a wild horse that could never be fully tamed. It was her wildness and her independence that drew him to her, he would say. Some men of that age felt their spouses "belonged" to their husbands, like chattel, but Anna and Charles belonged to each other. They were a part of each other.

Their first child was born in 1861 and they named her Elizabeth but always called her "Lizzie". More children were to come, boys who became strong and independent men. But Lizzie was the first and was favored. She would inherit the best traits of both Anna and Charles but like Anna there was an independent streak that was well accepted in the Lakota culture but would always mark her as different in white society. The country had endured a Civil War and after a time the migration west continued as it had before the war. Change was coming. Just four years after the end of the conflict, the golden spike was driven in the rail bed of the Transcontinental Railroad linking the two coasts. But the in between was now being populated, driven in part by speculators selling land to prospective immigrants from Germany, Scandinavia and other parts of Europe, the "Old World". This was news to the first Americans that their land, the land upon which they were born, upon which their ancestors had lived and died, that they now occupied, lived, hunted and civilized was being offered to future farmers and ranchers and their families living thousands of miles away. Unlike the culture of the white settlers, these lands had no paper deed or charter from the government to the Native Americans, they were just their lands. What would come was a clash.

The lure of open lands would drive many from across the ocean and others from the crowed Northeast and yet others disposed by the conflict of the Civil War to uproot and bring their families to the plains. Many came for farming and ranching. Others came seeking a place to raise their families. But the lure of open lands would never create the frenzy that the discovery of a shiny golden mineral in the Black Hills would have. Change would come and it would not be slow.

Charles had encouraged Anna to learn the skill of reading English which she had done. She could speak in one language while thinking in her native Lakota tongue. While books proved a wonder to practice her new skill, nothing proved as educational as the newspapers that reported the latest news. She had followed the reports of all the major battles of the Civil War and the passage of the Constitutional Amendments following the end of the war. But of greater interest she followed the conflicts between the newly arrived immigrants to the plains and the Lakota and other tribes leading to many deaths, retaliation and military intervention to crush the resistance of tribes to incursions into their lands. Finally in 1868 as a result of a Congressional study to reduce conflict between the federal government and the various tribes of Native Americans, a treaty was reached in Fort Laramie in Wyoming between the Sioux tribes and the US Government. Under that treaty the Sioux would be forced to yield claims to lands and agree to settle in Indian territory that included the sacred Black Hills in the Dakotas. By treaty this Indian Territory would be exclusive lands held by the tribe. The newspapers Anna read suggested that now, maybe there would be peace. She thought, now the lands of her Lakota ancestors would continue to be preserved and held sacred by those generations that followed. But her hopes would be dashed by the glory seeking of a golden blonde hero of the Civil War and the golden metal that his expedition would find in the Black Hills.

Anna sat there that October evening more than four and a half decades later staring at the moon and began to think back to 1875 and thought that it was a night like this that she made a fateful decision. It was the warrior spirit in her that drove the decision. She had lived with the white people long enough to know that, more than having gold, the idea of gold was the most powerful motivator driving society. Oh, the

Lakota liked what gold could do to adorn their bodies and decorate their tipis but they never craved the idea of gold like these people from the east. No law or treaty nor well intentioned federal government could stop the crazed people that would stop at nothing to get their share of that gold. And it had started the year before, in 1874, when George Custer lead an expedition into the very territory that had been ceded by the Fort Laramie Treaty to the Sioux, the Black Hills. The expedition proved what had been speculated in the newspapers for several years now. There was gold in the Black Hills and the Sioux were standing in the way of riches for the common folks.

Following the confirmation that gold was indeed in the Black Hills, prospectors came from far and wide leading, in 1875 and 1876, to a huge gold rush and the inevitable conflict between the Lakota and those seeking a fortune. This is not to say that there was a prolonged period of peace before the gold rush. There was Indian warfare throughout the post Civil War period but the spark for this period of war was the intrusion into the Black Hills. Anna and her daughter Lizzie followed the news reports with alarm as they understood that, treaty or not, the Black Hills were going to be forever changed. Their quiet talks went on for days. "How could this happen?", they asked each other. They could just let it pass. After all they were just a mother and daughter. They were like small pebbles in river. They could not stop the water. They had no right to affect the actions that the government could take. Where they lived was not even a state in America and even if it was, women had no say in government. Maybe some day they could convince the menfolk to act the same way women thought they thought they should. These were not those times. These were not ideas their menfolk could relate to. The notion of sacred land was foreign to those interested in cultivating the soil and possessing title to land through a deed or land grant. The idea that the Native Americans had some right equal to them was ridiculous. After all these people claiming the sacred lands were heathens and uncivilized. So Anna could not be heard. Lizzie understood that and saw her mother frustrated. Anna thought of the Lakota heritage that she had received from her Ina and felt she had to do something. Letting this pass was not an option. She confided in Lizzie, then nearly 15, that she would leave the home she and Charles had made, find the Redbear clan of her Ina and resist the invasion of the gold seekers. Lizzie listened and said, "I am going with you. We have to do something. If we do nothing the Black Hills will never be the same."

That night they placed their things in a blanket and tied it over their shoulders and left the Marshall home. Anna and Lizzie left a note explaining they were going to resist and try to make a difference. Anna knew her boys would be fine with Charles and she would take care that

Lizzie would be safe. They took one horse called Paint from the coral and set off towards Pine Ridge. Anna remembered much that her Ina had taught her about what they could eat from the land and how it should be prepared and cooked. Because of this when they arrived at Pine Ridge, neither was hungry.

Now, nearly forty-four years later, Anna sat and reflected on what she and her daughter had done. From the kitchen of the big house, Lizzie saw Anna smoking her pipe and looking at the stars in the light of the full moon and walked out the door and sat down with Anna and put her arm around her. They were both thinking and remembering how it was so many years before. Lizzie put her hand to Anna's chin and turned her head towards her and said, "we were warriors and we took a stand then and we fought. They came to take our sacred land and destroy our culture. We fought bravely. We made a difference and because of it many survived and we lived to tell our story. It is worth telling that story to those that follow us." Then as she returned to the house she turned and saw Anna lift her feet up and down and turn around while looking up to the heavens. Lizzie nodded knowingly. She is dancing in memory of those days.

In Pine Ridge Lizzie was introduced to the Redbear clan who listened carefully to the news that Anna and Lizzie had brought about the pending gold rush. That night the whole clan took their tipis down and set out west to find the gathering warriors who sought to defend the Black Hills and take back what the invaders had taken. The journey took them west of what was Dakota territory into Wyoming where the Cheyenne and the Sioux had gathered. Anna and Lizzie had traveled over 500 miles on this journey, accompanied by Paint, but mostly by foot. This place was near the Crow reservation, near the Big Horn River. The settlement included Sioux from both the Lakota and Dakota nations as well as Cheyenne, Arapaho and Crow. Anna and Lizzie joined the Lakota tribe along with their clan. As women, their jobs were well defined. They were called upon to gather food, prepare and cook for the tribe, to sew and mend clothing, to find suitable materials to make shafts for arrows, to sharpen the edges of knives and tomahawks. At night the women encouraged the warriors with their chanting and song, praising them for their bravery and calling upon the spirits to give them strength. Lizzie watched as Anna joined the women dancing to the drums and chanting. The whole encampment knew that the Army was on the way. From the south the soldiers had driven a band of Cheyenne out of the Powder River Basin in March 1876. Three months later, on June 17, the Lakota, and the Northern Cheyenne met the Army and its Indian allies from the Crow and Shoshone tribes at the Battle Rosebud Creek in Montana Territory. The Cheyenne called the battle the Battle "Where the Girl Saved Her Brother". In that engagement, the Cheyenne and Lakota under the leadership of Crazy Horse defeated General Crook. This defeat wrecked the Army strategy of sending three distinct columns into the Montana Territory and pinning the tribes between them. Custer was under the command of General Terry who marched his column from Fort Abraham Lincoln. The third column was the Montana Column commanded by Gibbon from Fort Ellis in the Montana Territory. The defeat would delay Crook's forces considerably frustrating the Army's plan to envelop the Sioux and Cheyenne near the Big Horn River.

In the course of the battle at Rosebud Creek, according to oral histories of the battle, an Indian women saved her wounded brother who was a Chief helping to rally the warriors in battle. Her actions were sung around campfires, inspiring all for battles to come. In a battle to the death between fierce adversaries, women fought side by side the male warriors. The women knew their fate in defeat and were fierce combatants. These tales were passed on to the women and men encamped at Greasy Grass as they prepared for battle. Lizzie and Anna wanted to know how they could help. They knew how to shoot a rifle but Anna and Lizzie had brought no rifles with them from their home. Less than a majority of the Sioux warriors had a repeating rifle. Single shot rifles were useful in hunts but in warfare the bow and arrow was a more effective weapon in the hands of the Sioux and Cheyenne warriors. They were more accurate astride a horse, at a close range, than the soldiers shooting a fire arm while mounted. Anna and Lizzie could expect no rifle to shoot in any battle. They learned their role was to ride with the warriors with supplemental arrows to resupply them while they chased and circled. the soldiers. They understood why the Lakota and Cheyenne had an advantage. Riding bareback without the weight of a heavy saddle, on unshod, nimble horses bred for speed, the Sioux and Cheyenne would prove to be hard targets for troopers trying to shoot rifles that were not rapid fire arms. The spirits of the Native Americans were high because they fought well mounted on horseback, but their motivation to defend their lands and culture was greater.

Just 8 days after the defeat at Rosebud Creek, General Terry ordered Lt. Colonel Custer to take the 7th Calvary to scout and determine where Sitting Bull and Crazy Horse were encamped. This was a splintering of Terry's force which Custer compounded when he further divided his force into three groups, one headed by Reno, the second led by Bentene and Custer leading the main force. They had their Native American scouts to assist them in this endeavor and in short order they had discovered parts of the encampment and the first group, under Reno was detached to attack with the second under Bentene continuing towards a further group of tipis. The warriors were largely gone from both of these encampments and had been alerted of the march of the 7th Calvary toward their villages. Those left in the encampment and the women put up a spirited fight defending their village and these fights kept the three units from presenting a unified fighting unit.

Anna and Lizzie had gone ahead with the force led by Sitting Bull and Crazy Horse, loaded with their arrows and riding astride horses. Warriors escaping from the villages had reported that that Custer's troopers had attacked them and were not far off from the Greasy Grass encampment.

As they awaited the soldiers, Lizzie looked down at the hands holding the reserve bundle of arrows. They were crusted with dirt and mud from all the work she had done preparing for this. But under that dirt, she knew, her skin was white, just as the soldiers that were on their way. Even her mother was not full blooded Lakota but she stood resolute with all gathered to resist. Could she really be part of this conflict that would probably result in death and injury to those troopers that looked more like her beneath all the dirt that covered her hands? She was not there to begin a fight or to cause a fight. She was not invading the lands of those with the same skin as hers. She was there to stand firm against the invaders, against those intending to kill those related to her, not just the warriors but even the women, including her mother and her. No she had no second thoughts now. This is what she and her mother had intended to do. She sat astride Paint and waited.

There are many versions of what happened that morning. History it seems is written by the victors, not of a battle, but of a war. This battle was a clear victory for Sitting Bull and Crazy Horse where they surrounded about 250 of Custer's force and killed every one of the troopers. Because no one of Custer's force was left alive in a battle fought to the death, it was forever known as a massacre. At the end of the day, there were heroes on all sides.

Anna and Lizzie after doing their best to resupply the warriors, returned to the encampment, helped move what could be transported and left with the Sioux and Cheyenne. There was little time for celebration. They knew other troopers were coming. After witnessing the deaths of so many, Anna and Lizzie, riding Paint and another pony Anna had ridden all day, separated from the mass exodus with some food and their belongings and turned east. Fifteen days later they returned home. They had agreed not to reveal what they had done and seen. Charles and Anna's sons were so happy to see them they never complained about their absence or probed too hard for the specifics about where they had been or what they had been doing. The whole countryside, indeed the whole nation, knew, by the time Anna and Lizzie arrived at home, of Custer's massacre.

Now forty-four years after their return they sat together again for the second time that evening, Anna smoking her pipe and Lizzie with her arm around Anna's shoulder. They talked about those days when they were standing up for the rights of the Lakota. Yes, the Lakota and Cheyenne had defeated Custer but the end was near as tribe after tribe surrendered. They followed what had happened after the final surrender of the Sioux. The treaties were not honored; the reservations they were assigned to were minuscule compared with the size of the territory covered by the Laramie Treaty of 1868; and the children were sent to Indian Schools like Carlisle, Pennsylvania and forced to give up their language, their customs, their religion and even their names. All was done to conform to what the whites called "being civilized". Somehow, the very things that Anna and Lizzie had left home to prevent had happened anyway. What they had preserved was their family and they had retained their fighting spirit that they held to this day.

Lizzie said she needed to go into the house because it was getting close to the time when her daughter Helen Irene was due to give birth and her husband Martin would need to be relieved shortly. Anna nodded and Lizzie went inside, still looking back, watching Anna gazing at the moon and listening. Though her eyes were weak with age, Anna was nearly 80 now, her ears were sharp. She heard every sound: every creature moving about, whether it was the animals in the barn or the deer calling to their mates; the flight of the evening owl; the movement of the breeze and the stirring in the farm house up the hill. She even thought she could hear the moon itself calling to her, whispering to her that a great thing would happen that night. What was it saying? The moon repeated its whisper, a great warrior would come tonight. She knew what the moon was saying.

Though Anna and her daughter Lizzie had shared much during the few months they had had ridden with her clan fighting the invading white soldiers, they were different. Anna was short in stature and Lizzie was tall. Anna was dark in complexion, with her black hair now silver in color. Lizzie was fair, her hair still blonde and full. Her features were passed to her by her father Charles, to whom Anna was married now for 60 years. Although Anna loved him still as much as the day she first cast eyes on him, she had settled in her ways, keeping many of her Lakota customs and manners and now living apart from him. Her daughter Lizzie was taught not only the ways of the Lakota but the ways of her father and had, following her return from the Sioux Wars, embraced them. Although she understood the spiritual beliefs of her mother, Lizzie had accepted the Catholic faith of Charles. This had not troubled Anna. She wanted only her happiness and could not have been prouder, than when Lizzie had married one of the leading businessmen in Bonesteel, Sam Lindley. Anna had not only lived to see Lizzie grow into a beautiful woman and become a successful businesswoman in her own right but Anna had witnessed the birth of Lizzie!s daughter Helen Irene Lindley. Anna had chosen to live the last decade in this hut behind Lizzie's large house. There she split her time helping raise Helen and working with Charles at his trading store. Helen Irene, Lizzie's only child, favored her grandmother in stature and skin tone. Where Lizzie was fair, Helen was darker in complexion with black hair. Throughout her life Helen Irene wore her hair short rather than long in the style of many of Native American Heritage. She had a determination that was evident to whomever met her. She knew what she wanted to achieve and what it would take to get there. But she had a gentle disposition and a wonderful sense of humor and an infectious laugh that once started would cause everyone nearby to join in. Tremendously curious, with a desperate need to learn as much as she could, she read everything in sight. She saw the independent nature of her mother and grandmother and long chaffed at the notion that women were second class citizens in America lacking the right to vote. It had been her cause and her fight. Maybe if Anna and Lizzie had had the right to vote years before, they could have had a say in how the Sioux were treated years ago.

Anna had watched Helen grow into a woman full of grace and charm and now married and with a child on the way. She had seen this child coming and heard from the moon that the child would be a great warrior and her heart had jumped for joy. Life would carry on. Anna could rest in peace. Her clan would continue. Anna reminisced about how her daughter had grown up after returning from the Sioux Wars and how her granddaughter had become a mother to be.

CHAPTER 2

LIZZIE AND HELEN IRENE

S taring at her mother through the kitchen window, she wondered what Anna was really thinking and thought about what was to come that evening. She had spent her entire life in the plains and had survived. In that period from her birth in 1864 to now the end of the second decade of the 1900's the world had changed, maybe more dramatically than in any era of America. The developments were dramatic and helped shape the country but more was to come.

The Civil War ended and the promise of improved civil rights was made but not kept. For many former slaves, the right to vote turned illusory with many laws enacted in the South virtually precluding the newly enfranchised from voting. While the African Americans formerly in bondage had the right in theory to vote, women had no constitutional right to vote and the movement to change that status was escalated with the end of the Civil War. But technology was never asleep and unbound by legislative restraints that limited humankind. Following the end of the war, the country was linked at Provo Utah joining the East and West coasts by rail. Thus, the two main ways to California and the West coast by ship or wagon across thousands of miles of hostile territory no longer were the preferred method of transportation, passenger transport or mail. Telegraph had long replaced the pony express as the quickest method of communications. The power of electricity was unleashed and although rural America would not be generally electrified until after the Great Depression in the 1930's, the major cities were filled with lights and buildings powered with electricity. Elevators were developed allowing buildings to rise into the sky without the time consuming and exhausting climb up several stories of stairs. Oil had been discovered and which allowed the general population to light their homes before electricity was practical. Telephones were invented and eventually reached rural America. Radio and phonographs were developed along with the automobile and flight. Commerce thrived and fashion changed. Sears and other retailers found ways to sell their wares to those in the Midwest through catalogs and traveling salesmen. People could even buy a prefabricated Craftsman home shipped to them by rail with instructions on how to successfully assemble the home without too many extra unaccounted for pieces. Traveling photographers would arrive by wagon or auto and set up shop, offering professional family photos and personal portraits. Many of these have been preserved and document what life was like in the last half of the 19th Century and now during the first two decades of the 20th Century.

But life in the plains was harsh and life expectancy was short due to disease, water quality and diet. Medicine and the availability of doctors who could treat diseases with real scientific solutions was limited. Loss of life in childbirth was a regular occurrence, with expectant mothers dying from complications or babies not surviving birth itself or lack of basic immunizations from childhood diseases. There were few hospitals outside the urban areas of America and complicated births resulted in disastrous results where doctors were not available or properly trained. Immigration exploded throughout the country but the lure of open land and the desire to attract investment through land which was purchased sight unseen or even by lottery was a joint effort by the federal and territorial governments. Vast portions of land were settled in former Indian Territories like Oklahoma through free-for-all land rushes which allowed migrants to claim land if they homesteaded it for the requisite period. Chicago became the second largest city in America by 1890. It would become the place to go for most of the Mid Westerners, even those in South Dakota. South Dakota and North Dakota, both formed out of the original Dakota Territory became states in 1889 despite their small populations.

Anna had given birth many times and Lizzie could see that it had taken its toll on her both in giving birth and the energy of raising a house full of children. Lizzie had learned early on, as the oldest, she was expected to help raising the family and she understood the demands and the risks of motherhood. But she saw the other side of life. When she was not in the home behind the store, she was working the counter in the trading store or stocking the shelves with trade goods or keeping track of inventory. She was as interested in pricing the goods to make a reasonable profit as she was in greeting long time customers. Anna kept the floors neat and clean and mostly stayed out of sight. Few customers really understood that Anna, an Indian, was Charles' wife. But everyone knew Lizzie and were happy to trade with her and her father even though there were other competing establishments in Bonesteel.

Lizzie was constantly improving the business to increase sales. She was the first to notice the Sears Catalog offering cash registers for sale and ordered one without even understanding how it worked. When customers saw that the register recorded the sale price for an item and tallied all the purchases, they flocked to the store. Quickly she began to label prices on merchandise to make the customer assured they were getting an accurate price for the goods. Charles had great confidence in the innovations Lizzie made but worried that she was so devoted to the store that she would never find a suitable husband.

Of course Lizzie was interested in finding the proper husband, but knew it would happen when it was the right time. Just as she was thinking about the next shipment of trade goods, in walked a big cocky Englishman with an Irish brogue accent looking for goods for a new home he was building in town. A bachelor, newly arrived in Bonesteel via London, New York and Chicago, Sam Lindley was duly impressed by this sophisticated and modern store this far away from Chicago and New York. He inquired of Lizzie how the cash register was acquired and who had decided to make the acquisition. Lizzie looked him in the eye and said, "I made the decision. It has made a difference in sales." He understood this was not a hobby for her but a business and she was in charge, though the name on the store was the "Charles Marshall Trading Post." Lizzie introduced herself and was immediately impressed with Sam's interest in her business acumen and how he treated her as an equal.

Samuel Lindley was born in 1860 and was just a little older than Lizzie and saw that many immigrants were flocking to the Midwest to make new lives. Many were from Germany, Scandinavia, and England and Ireland. He felt that these newcomers would need capital to purchase or expand their homesteads, purchase livestock or seeds for planting. He, being a newcomer himself, felt that these new arrivals would feel more comfortable with borrowing at a bank established with them in mind. During his planning stages for this new business he would stop in and pick Lizzie's brain for ideas on how to attract the kind of customers that she saw coming into the Marshall store. She was happy to talk with Sam and felt that he was impressed with her ideas and encouragement. She appreciated that he treated her as an equal which was not the norm in society at that time. That was important to her. For most men, women were just that, women, and second class members of society at that. It was clear to her that Sam was going some place and would soon take a high place in town society. But she did not think about that, he was just her friend Sam. Then, seemingly out of the blue, he asked her to marry him. She thought a moment and said, "I have to talk with you a moment and then let you think about whether you want to ask me that question." She said that the woman in the back room cleaning was her mother. "Her name is Anna Brazos Marshall and she is half Lakota, or as they say hereabouts, Sioux," she said. "In this country there is an expression, 'a single drop of blood'. It means that I am Sioux too as far as many are concerned and my children and their children and so on will be deemed and treated by many as Sioux. So you are asking if a Sioux will marry you. If that is acceptable to you, you may ask me again. If not, I will not hold it against you if you refrain." Sam reached across the counter and took her hand and said, "I want to marry you even more. You are the most honest and forthright woman I have ever met and I want to spend all my days with you if you will have me." A month later they were married at the Immaculate Conception Catholic Church in Bonesteel, her mother and father sitting in the first pew.

Sam had agreed that Lizzie could continue to manage the Marshall trading store as long as she wanted but that she would have social obligations as the wife of a leading banker in Bonesteel. She began to dress more elegantly and entertain frequently as her home became one of the social centers of Bonesteel. The transition from fast friends to intimate lovers was easy for Sam and Lizzie. They were deeply in love and within a few months Lizzie was expecting and due in August of 1898.

In the beginning of 1898, tensions between Spain and the United States about interests in Cuba and Puerto Rico became tense. Some in America felt that expansion was a good thing but wars were expensive. But all that changed when the battleship Maine was destroyed in Havana Harbor, Cuba in 1898. That led to a declaration of war against Spain even though there was no direct proof that Spain had deliberately attacked the ship. One of the key military leaders in the war with Spain in Cuba was Theodore Roosevelt of New York who had spent valuable time in the 1880's in the Dakotas hunting and cultivating his interests in conservation, eventually building a home in Elkhorn, North Dakota. The time spent in the Dakotas not only shaped his belief in conservation, it did wonders for his frail condition, his strength and self-confidence. Roosevelt raised a group of volunteers called the Rough Riders which played a prominent role in the victory in Cuba. The war was brief and decisive and resulted in the independence of Cuba and the island of Puerto Rico becoming a territory of the United States along with the Philippines. The war had a small impact on the economy of the Midwest but the rise to national prominence led to Roosevelt becoming McKinley's running mate in the 1900 Presidential election and Roosevelt becoming President when McKinley was assassinated in September 1901.

The war with Spain did not change the world for Lizzie's only child Helen Irene Lindley. The war was over almost before it began. But change would continue in the Midwest and throughout the country. A new spirit of progressive thought was coming. Lizzie was proud to have a daughter but knew as a woman in the Dakotas, she would grow up a second class citizen. She vowed that in Helen Irene's lifetime that would change if Lizzie had anything to do with it. Lizzie was glad that she had disclosed her Sioux heritage prior to her engagement as Helen' appearance and stature would favor Anna. Her beauty was unquestioned but she did not have the fair skin of her mother. In some respects, being a women was as big a handicap in life as being of Indian descent. Make up, dress and speech could overcome the stigma of Native American relations, but a woman was still a woman.

Helen Irene grew up in a deeply religious, loving, household that encouraged and supported education. Her parents supported the local schools to raise their standards and by the time of Helen's graduation, her high school was one of the better high schools in the state. Both Lizzie and Sam were active in the support of the Suffragette movement in South Dakota and would introduce Helen to the key activists in the state. The trouble with the movement was that many supporting the movement were also part of the temperance movement which if successful could affect the profits at the Marshall store. Until the movement stood by itself, it would be difficult to win the day.

When Helen Irene was 16, Sam and Lizzie decided to take her on a road trip for her birthday. Sam had bought a new Model T Ford and thought a trip to the big city would be the trip of a lifetime. They packed their bags and set off. Over the years between Sam's banking contacts and Lizzie's relationships with suppliers for the Marshall store, they had mapped out a route that allowed them to stop and visit folks along the way, spending several nights with friends and a few distant relatives all the while locating the few fuel points that had been established along the main routes. A handy spare gas can kept them from running out. The roads, mere wagon trails really, were dusty and rough but, without exception everyone they met along the way was friendly and hospitable.

It was great adventure that was made all the more meaningful because the little family was not interrupted by the time-consuming work that Helen's mom and dad did that absorbed all their time. The sights were memorable and by the time they got to the outskirts of Chicago, Helen felt she knew her parents better than ever before. Helen took in all the sites and enjoyed the architecture. Buildings were getting taller every year. She and her parents took a sailboat ride in Lake Michigan and ate at some fabulous steakhouses and she went into the kitchens of several restaurants to learn some of the recipes that she would keep her whole life. But as interested in culinary matters as Helen was, the most momentous event that occurred during the family's visit to Chicago was the meeting Lizzie had arranged with the leaders of the Suffragette movement in their offices in the Monadnock Building, then the tallest building in Chicago. The whole family was present in the session and listened to the leaders talk about the importance of the proposed amendment to the Constitution that had was being discussed in many states including South Dakota. It was an effort that dated back to the 1840's and both Helen and Lizzie were energized by the words and understood the importance of doing whatever they could in their own state to assure passage of the amendment. It was a memorable trip and Helen would talk of it for many years. Helen was determined to make sure that any daughter she would bring into the world some day, would have the sacred right to vote. But she knew, and Lizzie had reinforced it when they talked, that the men who held the power and who were being petitioned to approve the amendment held ancient beliefs. They referenced the Bible as a source that men should govern and that women should be subservient. They believed that women did not have the brains to deal with politics; they were too emotional and not fact driven. They believed that if a husband felt that a party or candidate was the one to vote for, no wife should have the right to contradict the husband's point of view. *Further if the women had the right to vote, they would seek public office and those in power were threatened by this possibility.* Lizzie and Helen explored all the arguments that would be raised during the approval process for the Nineteenth Amendment and understood how difficult the battle would be. *Power once held would not be relinquished easily. It would prove to be a reality a century later.*

Helen's family returned to Bonesteel and along the way back, Sam taught her to drive the Model T and she felt proud of her accomplishment but had longed to return to the home and ride her own horse Bella. When they reached home that afternoon in early September, Helen ran to the coral and called Bella who came trotting over as excited to see Helen as Helen was to see her. Bella had the same markings as Paint, the horse that Anna and Lizzy had ridden off to the Sioux Wars. Helen saddled Bella and took off for a long ride into town. As much as she was excited to be riding Bella, she was looking forward to riding over to her boyfriend Martin's house more. Helen and Martin had grown up as neighbors and educated at the same schoolhouse and now high school and went to Church together at Immaculate Conception. Martin Schonebaum was a little older than Helen but she had attracted his attention with her intellect and good looks. Helen was captivated by his strawberry blonde hair which he always kept well groomed, his warm personality and his determination to make something of himself. He was going to the University and planned to study law and had been working and saving to make that happen. Helen herself had planned to attend the University and would be, if admitted, the first woman from Bonesteel to attend and the first woman of Native American descent to be accepted. Her mother and father had groomed her and encouraged Helen to pursue a college degree. While she was focused on college, Helen became more and more smitten with Martin. In his last year of high school, she spent as much time with him as possible. They loved to sit out on the hill overlooking Martin's farm, holding hands and looking at the sky and talking about the future. Helen told him all about her trip to the big city of Chicago. Martin had never been east of Sioux Falls, South Dakota and was very interested in everything about her trip. He had seen the new auto that Sam had bought and was interested in everything about it. Martin had been very impressed that Helen had driven back from Chicago. He listened as she talked about the meeting with the leaders of the Suffragette movement and the grand meals in the hotels in the big City. Hearing these things, did not make Martin envious but fired his determination to make something of himself and accomplish something great in the eyes of Helen if she would ever have him. He thought of these things as they lay there side by side holding hands and looking at the heaven. He thought about all the arguments that Helen had suggested would be raised against the Nineteenth Amendment and thought about his own experiences. He had studied the Bible throughout his life and could think of nothing that suggested that women could not vote. His own experiences with women in his life confirmed his opinion that women were strong not weak, were often far brighter than many menfolk, and were far more interested and passionate about political causes than many of the men he knew. Moreover, how could it be justified to keep the most significant right from anybody just because of their gender. It was just wrong. He had agreed with everything she and he had talked about but he did feel that if he owned an auto, he would drive rather than Helen. Helen and Martin separated as Martin went off to the University and Helen finished her High School studies. Their love continued but geography was in the way.

It was her Senior year in high school and Helen Irene was notified that she had been accepted into the University beginning September 1916. There she would attend classes and hopefully resume her deep friendship with Martin who would begin his last year of undergraduate studies. Lizzie was thrilled that Helen would attend college, a dream that Lizzie had since her birth. Lizzie had arranged for a graduation celebration at the Immaculate Conception church hall and had invited Martin to attend as a surprise. She even brought Bella to the party though she was now too old to do much but eat grass and wander about in the pasture but age had not diminished her beauty. Helen was so surprised to see Martin and Bella too. She peppered Martin with questions about the University and what she should do over the summer to prepare and then she went to Bella and stroked her face knowing that maybe this time next year Bella would be alive. Bella nuzzled against Helen's hand and seemed to agree.

Helen and Martin talked about the future and their role in it. Martin could tell that Helen was still as determined as ever to win the right to vote for women. He pointed out that the University was a very male oriented institution and that she would be the first to change that.

Moreover, he advised that few of her fellow students would agree with her views on the right to vote. Helen was not surprised and pointed out that that was precisely the environment she would want to become immersed in. Each day will give me a new challenge to practice my arguments in favor of my view and allow me to persuade them to my point of view. "This will be very exciting", she said.

CHAPTER 3

HELEN AND MARTIN

Not only was Helen Irene the first woman from Bonesteel to attend South Dakota University but she was the first of Sioux descent to attend. She knew from her mother that emphasizing her heritage would not help her succeed in her studies. So the last words of wisdom that her mother gave her as she boarded the train to Vermillion was that she should act white and ignore the bigotry that was surely present in a collage that did not encourage Native American applicants. When she got off the train in Vermillion, Martin was there to greet her. He hugged and kissed her as they greeted and was as excited to see her as she was to see him. Martin picked up her bags and walked her to the boarding house where she would spend four years living while at the University. As there were no dormitories for female students, she had taken a room in a boarding house near campus owned by Mrs. Gertrude Englehart. There she had her meals and could study when she was not in the Library. Martin, who was finishing his last year at the University, would begin his studies at the recently completed law school at South Dakota!s University.

Helen, despite her many hours of study, attended all of Martin's track races in his Senior year. He was a strong runner and his slight build make him well suited for the sport. She treasured his yearbook picture of Martin in his track uniform. Martin finished his undergraduate studies and began law school. But events in Europe would interrupt his studies part way through. As his undergraduate major was in European studies, Martin had closely followed the events in Europe since 1914. The assassination of Archduke Ferdinand and his wife had been the flashpoint to the Great War that saw Germany, Austria and Turkey pitted against Britain, France, the low countries, Italy and Russia. The United States was dominated by isolationists and public opinion was conflicted between anti and pro German and anti and pro British groups. Others wanted to see America become a great power. Some felt that war would be as easy as the Spanish American and the victories in Cuba. Further, the country was ill prepared for any war that was outside the continental US. In fact the only standing Army had spent the last few years chasing the bandit Pancho Villa in Mexico. That armed conflict provided combat experience for some but the campaign was not the success that Wilson had hoped for. But others pointed out that we could not even catch and defeat Pancho Villa in Mexico. How could we hope to win if we got involved in Europe. The country was simply divided.

President Wilson had campaigned for reelection in 1916 on the political platform of keeping the United States out of the Great War. He took this position despite the sinking of the Lusitania in 1915 and clear evidence that the unrestricted German submarine war on British shipping cost American lives. He was elected to a second term keeping America out of war. But Germany overplayed its hand and was not content with having America on the sidelines. Germany continued its unrestricted submarine warfare on commercial shipping crossing the Atlantic ocean.

Shipping belonging to Britain and countries that were fighting Germany were fair game even if the vessels were not armed. The risk of killing citizens of neutral countries like America was worth it to Germany if it shortened the war. Moreover, Germany took the position that so called neutral countries that traded with countries at war with

Germany were aiding the enemy and were also fair game to having their shipping sunk. Now Germany was pushing its luck by threatening to sink American flagged ships heading to England and France.

Germany knew that submarine warfare was working and the threat of directly attacking American vessels might work as well as actually attacking any ships. But the German government still felt the need to strike a more convincing blow. Perhaps, officials thought, if Germany could create a distraction, the United States would be kept on the sidelines. Germany sent communications to their Ambassador to the United States about the concept of talking the Mexican Government into declaring war on the United States with German support. Their reward would be the restoration of Mexican territories lost to the United States 70 years earlier. The cable was intercepted by the US and once disclosed, Wilson had no choice but to ask Congress for a formal declaration of war against Germany and its allies. America was at war with Germany.

Martin was a German American. His father August Schonebaum was a second generation American and his mother the former Anna Kappleman, was born in Germany and had migrated to America with her parents following the attractive homesteading offers of land speculators.Martin!s family had no quarrel with Germany. After all it was the homeland of both his parent!s families. But many in South Dakota, even some of German descent, were incensed by the unprovoked attack of American shipping and the fact that in their part of the state there were so many wealthy German American families caused tension. Even though their neighbors knew their families well, there still was unspoken resentment for the Schonebaums, particularly Martin's German speaking mother Anna Kappleman Schonebaum. The fact that she had been in America almost fifty years did not shield the family from the stares and snide remarks about possible German sympathies. Martin had received several letters from his mother about the resentment of the Schonebaum by some Bonesteel families. This was a dilemma for Martin.

Martin had a long series of discussions with Helen Irene and told her that he felt if he joined the Army he would be blunting any criticism of his family. While he did not wish to interrupt his law studies, he felt that service in the Army would probably help his law career. Moreover, the actions of Germany, notwithstanding his German ancestry, just could not be justified. Helen Irene supported his decision and the fact that her father had strong British sympathies made encouraging Martin easy.

Martin had studied European history at University and the possibility of fighting on European soil was definitely exciting. The quickest way he knew to get into the fight was to enlist in the South Dakota Army National Guard which the local Vermillion newspaper reported would be activated, trained and ready to depart for Europe well before any draftees. Martin went into the Guard depot and signed up, after passing a perfunctory physical. He had pocketed his glasses so that the sergeant did not notice his nearsightedness. He was told to report in a week in Sioux Falls at the train station and meet up with his Guard Unit there. He went back to school, informed his professors, said his goodbyes to his classmates and spent a few days walking around the campus with Helen Irene. They talked about the future and how their lives would be changed by the war and how they hoped their lives would be when he returned. They talked about family and country and how important it was to stand up to the country that had attacked theirs. Helen Irene told Martin that she had volunteered with the local Red Cross and was planning to do her part in support of the Country. Martin wrote letters to his parents telling them of his enlistment and the desire he had to serve his Country. His letter was short and he showed it to Helen Irene before he mailed it.

Dear Mother and Father,

I want to tell you that I have enlisted in the South Dakota Army National Guard and will be leaving Sioux Falls on Saturday for training in preparation for fighting against the armies of Germany in Europe. I know a few guys in the troop and I am certain that I am doing the correct thing joining in this fight. Helen Irene believes in me and has told me so. I wanted you both to know I intend to marry her as soon as this war is over. She is the most important thing in my life next to you both and it means a lot to me to know that I have her blessing for me to join this great cause. I hope and pray that I have yours too.

Your son,

Martin

At the same time, Helen Irene wrote to Lizzie:

Dear Lizzie,

My dearest mother, I am so happy and I want to share it with you and Father. Martin and I have been following all the events that have caused our country to declare war against Germany and Martin has joined the South Dakota Army National Guard. We have spent a great deal of time together this past week and Martin gained the courage to ask for my hand in marriage. I have accepted and we are to be wed after he returns from this terrible war. Martin is departing for training in California before going to France. It will be the farthest he has ever been from home. I promised to write him every day. Be happy for me and pray that Martin returns safe from war.

Love,

Helen L

That Saturday he got a train ride into Sioux Falls and met his troop. Because he had just enlisted, he was the only member of the troop that was not in uniform. The Company Commander gave him a used campaign hat and welcomed him to the adventure of a lifetime. Every trooper was issued a limb from a tree and told to carry it wherever they went. It was supposed to remind them that as a soldier, they were expected to carry a rifle whether they were training to be an infantryman, a clerk or a cook. "Never lose sight of your rifle. You will be trained with a real weapon later. But for now, treat this branch as you would your girlfriend. Love her and she will love you back," his company commander said. The train was filled with guardsmen, each with their tree limbs. The train departed Sioux Falls and headed south to Omaha following the Missouri River. At each stop, the guardsmen were ordered out of the train and drilled by the noncommissioned officers. The training had begun to prepare them for war. From his window seat, Martin watched the scenery roll by. A few farms made way for grazing herds of buffalo and deer feeding on the vast prairie of Nebraska. Periodically the train stopped to refuel the steam engine with wood and water. There provisions were also loaded on the train for the passengers. Mail was picked up in route to California. Every once in a while one of the troop bought a newspaper which the whole company read thoroughly, passing it carefully from seat to seat. The train moved into the Rocky Mountains and Martin felt he was close to heaven. He had seen the outcroppings of the Black Hills back in South Dakota but they were nothing compared to the majesty of the peaks of the Rockies. After three days of travel, he reached the training camp near San Diego. Then the fun began.

At camp he was issued a uniform that did not fit well and boots that were a little large and was issued a wooden rifle that worked as well as the limb he was issued in Sioux Falls. They were told that all would be issued a proper rifle later in training. In the meantime, the troopers ran carrying their make believe weapons over hills and through wooded valleys and streams. Martin loved running and usually finished well ahead of his platoon and company. The few weapons they trained on were relics and not up to the standards of those currently in use by either side in the conflict. Machine guns were demonstrated but no one was well trained on them either. They were being trained but they would not realize how poorly they were being prepared until they got to France. He wrote two letters at the end of his first week of training.

Father and Mother,

We have finished our first week of training here in the south of California. I cannot write about where we are training but we are living in tents and working hard. I think we will be here a few more weeks and then shipped east to another training post before leaving for the conflict. I am better prepared than most of the company because I can handle a rifle and am in good physical condition from all the running I did in school. I got your letter congratulating me on my engagement to Helen Irene and am grateful for your kind words. She is a wonderful girl and I know will make me very happy. But first we must fight and win this war and I will do my part.

Your loving son,

Martin

The second was to his future bride.

My dearest Helen,

I know from you last letter that you are worried for me but please do not be. I am well and in good hands of the commanders of our Army company. We are being trained to work together and follow our leaders commands. That is hard for some who have always done things their way. I treasure the few days we spent

31

together walking the campus and holding you in my arms. It was the happiest time of my life. I can close my eyes tonight and see you even now wearing the fashionable dress and holding the flowers I gave you and saying that you would wait for me and be my wife. It is a picture that I will never forget. It will carry me through the days before me. Do not worry for me. I know this war will take me far from you. But it will be over someday soon.

With God's help and your prayers,

I will return to you.

Love,

Martin.

CHAPTER 4

HELEN IRENE
THE GIRL AT HOME

After their whirlwind courtship at University and Martin had left to serve, Helen Irene began planning for life ahead. Life in Bonesteel prepared one to live simply. Women learned to cook and take care of the home and to do most of the domestic chores on a farm but Helen felt there was much more to life. While she loved the farming community, she had longed for a better life for her own family. Smart, petite with dark eyes and black hair which she always wore short, she preferred simple clothing although she could afford the latest in fashion. Helen was bright and well read. She had immersed herself in all her studies and hoped to be among the first female graduates of University of Sioux descent. Lizzie had long counseled her to ignore her Sioux heritage while pursuing her studies because of the prejudices that were deeply felt by many whites in the state. It was not difficult for Helen Irene to accentuate her white bloodlines for the English bred Lindley family name had opened up many doors in the small Bonesteel community. These doors were not open to her mother, Lizzie, when she came of age living with her parents. Helen Irene wanted more out of life than a farmer!s wife or even the proprietress of a trading store. Reading and studying at University opened her eyes to so many possibilities. But

Martin!s courtship of her had changed all that. She knew that Martin was interested in pursuing life as a lawyer and she spent many hours imagining what life as a lawyer!s wife would be like and what kind of family they would have together. What would their children look like and what kind of life would they have. But first she had to complete her studies at University. She knew though that her parents would question whether she should even finish school if she was going to marry Martin. She had listed all the reasons for completion in her mind and wrote a forceful letter to her parents. She just knew that Lizzie would support her goals and if she was behind her, her father would not disagree. She wrote again to her parents to lay out her case with the force of an experienced advocate.

Dear Lizzie and Father,

I am so happy that you approve of my marriage to Martin. We have always been close friends growing up and love each other!s company and see the future with the same pair of eyes. We don!t know how long this war will last so it!s too early to plan a wedding. I have already planned my subjects for the fall semester and am so looking forward to continuing my studies. I just know you want me to finish University because the future cannot be known. With a completed education, I can take a proper place in South Dakota. I believe that an educated wife is just going to help with Martin!s future in the law or whatever position he seeks after the war. I know he will come back to me after the conflict is over but you have raised me to be a strong independent woman. I can be that best if I continue my studies.

Your loving daughter,
Helen Irene

Helen had learned from her classmates that the local chapter of the Red Cross was seeking volunteers. Since she had no training in medicine or nursing, she gravitated to projects that would support soldiers like Martin and the other South Dakota boys serving the country. She attended meetings and discovered ways that she could send reminders of home to the serving troops as well as send things that would aid them in the fight. She joined a committee that worked to prepare care package for the troops to include soap, socks, scarves, head coverings and other toilet necessities. Books and magazines were collected along with issues of the hometown newspapers and general letters of support. These items were packaged and sent abroad and handed out to troops during the war. These packages were real boosts to troop morale, a touch of home and a reminder that people back home care about them. Excitedly, she wrote to Martin.

My darling Martin,

Oh Martin so much is going on here back in Bonesteel. The newspaper published a list of local men that were training in California with your division. Not only did they list your name but mentioned that you were a star athlete and had patriotically left your studies at the University to serve. How glorious! Your parents are so proud. I joined the local chapter of the Red Cross and have been sewing as well as wrapping packages that will be sent to soldiers like you when you are sent overseas. I don!t see how you would get the one that I wrapped but I marked mine with a buffalo so you would know it was from me.

I convinced my mother, you know she always takes my side, and father, that I just have to finish my studies at University. It is important that a wife of a future lawyer be properly educated. I spend much of my day doing chores around the farm and day dreaming of our life together when you return. Lizzie is trying to make me focus on the practical skills a future wife should possess. Father has been following the news reports of the war and is gathering maps of France and Belgium. Anna talks to me about war and the pain that follows. She spends her days hunched over her small fire in her grass hut behind our house offering prayers and chants that you will come home safe to me. Anna says that I must be brave so that you will be brave. I know how fearless you are but I will be brave for you.

All my love,

Helen Irene

It was nearing the end of Summer and it seemed that everyone was working to prepare for the early harvest and, for students especially, the return to classes. While the newspaper reported the news from the war, there was not too much that folks in South Dakota could understand. But Helen had been getting regular letters from Martin and knew much more than her neighbors did. Martin had written to her when he was shipped to train in Virginia and again when he got his orders to sail to France early in the Summer of 1917. He had seen the ship they would sail on and it was an old passenger ship that was repurposed for transporting soldiers to Europe. Helen knew that Martin was part of the Prairie division that was mostly National Guardsmen. Martin had chosen to remain an enlisted soldier and not volunteer to undergo further training to become an officer despite suggestions from his commanding officer. He did not want to leave his friends and delay his own departure for the war. He felt he could do his best with those he had trained with. Helen had gotten Martin's first letter after sailing to France nearly a month and a half after he had written it. Letters were shipped first to England and then to New York where everyone was reviewed for sensitive information. He had been careful to avoid sharing any information that the censors would flag, preventing parts of the letter to be blocked. He wanted to let her know he was then in Europe and that she should not worry. Even though he had sailed from Virginia, his ship had rendezvoused with other troop transports departing from New York. The journey had taken almost two weeks and even though they had done physical training on board, he knew that all of the soldiers would have to work to get into proper physical condition and really concentrate on advanced infantry training.

Dearest Helen,

I hope I do not have to sail again too soon. The voyage took us nearly two weeks as we sailed first north and then south, towards England and then to France. No one ate very well because we were very seasick. Even the sailors had a hard time keeping their food down. We headed to the closest port in France and marched off our ship and set up camp. Our officers told us the plan was to take trains east towards the front. Our supply companies had brought several locomotives and train cars in ships that had arrived before we did. They were some of the same train cars that had taken us across America to Virginia. But we learned that the train tracks in France were not the same size as American tracks so our locomotives and train cars were just sitting near the docks. So now we will do what soldiers do and that is march to the front. Actually, it will be a great experience because the French people are happy to see us and crowd the roads wherever we march cheering and waving French and handmade American flags. It is thrilling to hear the shouts.

I am safe and will be brave for you. I cherish your letters and you should know how much they mean to me. Many of my friends do not have anyone writing them and I share parts of your letters with them to cheer them up. They feel as if they know you as well as I do. Your letters will be sent to me even when I am ordered to the front if you send them to the return address on my letter.

Love,

Martin

CHAPTER 5

WE ARE HERE

Helen understood that Martin!s unit was among the first American forces that had arrived in France and that he would see action. Even so she understood that she would just not know for weeks after any battle what happened and who fought. Additionally, both Martin and her father Sam had explained that the war was being fought out of trenches, which were like furrows in farm fields deep enough for men to stand up in and fire their rifles across a muddy field at soldiers in deep cuts yards away. Throughout the first three years of the war, enemies occupied each other army!s trenches depending on the outcome of a battle. Back and forth the armies moved with death all around. American troops knew that this was what they could expect but that was a different kind of battle than Martin!s troopers had in mind. The Indian wars were fought as mobile battles with combatants moving and maneuvering.

Anna and Lizzie had explained the battles in the prairies. Trench warfare was a different kind of animal. Mud, filth and the dead filled the trenches and wire wrapped with razor sharp protrusions separated the forces. This wire, barbed wire, was unlike that seen in the American West used to separate one rancher's property from another and keep livestock from wandering away. Barbed wire was easily erected and allowed the enemy gunners to see through the wire and cut down advancing troops. As charging troops attempted to avoid piercing their flesh on the barbed wire or becoming totally entangled in it, they were gunned down by a new technology, rapid firing machine guns. The carnage was devastating.

Martin had written to Helen reporting that the first wave of American troops had ceremoniously announced that "Lafayette We Are Here". Both had been avid readers of American history and particularly the Revolutionary War. Martin knew the newspapers would pick up the American announcement but felt that he should share that with Helen Irene. He knew that the significance of what the American troops were doing would mean a lot to Helen Irene. The Prairie division that included Martin!s Company landed in the Port of Brest France which is located in Province of Brittany. It was the port in France closest to the United States. The troops quickly disembarked and encamped in fields outside of Brest. There they trained. There were large encampments outside Paris where Martin!s unit trained and became acquainted with the whole concept of trench warfare. Though the first units had received some training in America, the weapons they used were ancient and ammunition was short in supply. So live fire exercises were rare in their State-side training. The American Commanding General, John Pershing, was happy that the first elements of the American Expeditionary Force (AEF) had arrived but he had determined that few of his soldiers were trained sufficiently to fight the kind of war that the Great War had become. Much more would be required. He knew it would take months before a critical mass of US troops would be trained and transported to France but he would have to do with the few troops that had arrived early in the Summer of 1917. He also realized that with the French and British and Commonwealth troops having fought and suffered deaths and casualties, they viewed the arrival of the Americans with conflicting points of view. First, the Americans would be raw and inexperienced compared to the French and British armies. Second, both countries had suffered tremendous losses over the first three years of the war so any new soldiers would be a welcome relief. Third, the Americans were arriving into the rats nest of the constant bickering between the Allies about who is in command, the French or the British. Add to that the question festering between the French and the British was to whom would the American troops report. Should the organization of the American army be dismantled and the soldiers dispersed among the British and French armies much like replacements were being handled. Or would they be assigned company by company to the command units of the armies of Britain and France. Proficient use of rifles was not a high priority for either the British or French. Warm bodies that could wait in trenches for months and then participate in mass charges across the battlefields was all that both allies felt was necessary. Into this atmosphere, Pershing brought his strong views and was backed fully by the President. He was not a fan of prolonged trench warfare. Rather he felt that movement and attack was the type of warfare that suited the American soldier. He was determined that the American Army would be under his command and the command of his generals and officers. He expected to fight not under his Allies but alongside them, taking the full measure of the German Army. He did not pretend his Army was fully combat ready but he was committed to get them properly ready. In the meantime it was important to show his Allies that trained American troops could hold their own if not win battles that his allies might not be able to because they were war weary.

Pershing selected his best trained unit with the firepower that would support the Allied troops for a planned assault against the German line at St Mihiel near the Meuse River. The American role was to provide support to the infantry charge against the fortified trenched the Germans had held for over a year since the beginning of the war. Surprising to the Allied command, the American troops fearlessly overcame the heavy machine gun fire from the German line causing a route of the heavily fortified trenches and seized them. The Americans had made their mark and entered the war. They had not only arrived but they had convinced the Allied command that they would turn the tide. Martin and his recent arrivals were still training.

CHAPTER 6

ANNA'S DREAM

Anna loved Charles and had been faithful to him since her return from the Sioux Indian wars. But she could not live in the wooden house attached to the trading post. She loved the freedom of the open sky and the feel of the prairie beneath her feet. She continued each day to walk from her grass hut behind Lizzie!s home to the trading post to be with Charles and help with the business . Though she spent the whole day at the post, she remained in the background almost invisible to the trappers selling their furs to Charles and the customers that visited the post buying dry goods and trading their farm produce for needed supplies. It was a busy place but few who entered the post were aware that Anna was Charles wife and had been for nearly fifty years. Lizzie had long before taken over the day to day operations of the post, leaving her father Charles to putter around the store and talk to the old timers that seemed to show up each day. Many of them still wanted to talk about the battles with the Sioux as much as what was going on in France. Charles followed the news reports and had attached maps of France and Belgium on the wall near the potbellied stove that was the source of heat in the store in the colder months. Sam stopped in every now and then and shared his news and commented on the topography of the countries fighting it out in trenches. It was Indian

Summer now and the evenings were cool but the days mild. Winter would soon be approaching and Lizzie had already received the bulk of winter goods that she planned to sell when the weather changed. Lizzie turned her thoughts to France and how the weather would be getting cold there as well. She spent a lot of time studying the maps and reading the news reports. She understood and supported the American entry into the Great War and the fact that Helen Irene!s beloved Martin was involved in the battles being reported was an important reason to follow the events in France.

At the end of the day, Lizzie would drive her carriage back to her house and insist that Anna ride back with her. She would talk with Anna about the war and describe the horrible weapons that were being used against each other. Anna would listen intently and nod. She had understood warfare but did not understand all the horrors of gas and grenades and machine guns and long range rifles. But she appreciate that the white man was always coming up with new ways to kill and maim. Naturally, that would continue. Anna usually made no comment to Lizzie!s explanations except to inquire how Helen Irene was doing at the University and whether her heart was happy or saddened by Martin!s absence at war. Lizzie always shared Helen Irene!s letters with Anna which were always filled with joy and happiness. But she would reassure Anna that Helen Irene was not troubled by Martin!s absence nor fearful about the hazards of war. But Lizzie knew that Anna could sometimes see things that Lizzie could not. She reminded Lizzie that with winter close at hand, the warriors would need to keep warm. Lizzie nodded and wrote to Helen to make sure her Red Cross group would send warm things to Martin and the other soldiers.

Sometimes, Anna would spend long hours in the evening staring at the fire outside her hut without moving. She might chant a song or stare at the sky and the stars above. She would smoke her ancient pipe though she would mostly puff while she gazed at the sky. Then seemingly in a trance she would close her eyes and see. Sometimes she would see the battles of her youth riding bareback whooping and yelling in support of the mounted warriors defending her lands. Now in her vision there were no ponies, no painted warriors swooping down on cavalry dressed in blue.

Anna saw cannon flashing just as they did when she rode with the Lakota. The explosions frightened her then and she was startled at how real they sounded in her vision. She could see that a great battle was being waged. She saw soldiers in grey and some in green running from the sounds and many lying in the mud with their eyes open and staring up from the mud. Others were screaming with blood spread out over the ground. All she could do was stare in silence, stunned at the sight. What did it mean? What could she say about it when she did not even understand what the Great War was all about? She would talk about it with Lizzie. She had listened to many of Anna!s visions and could offer good counsel. Maybe Lizzie could tell her what it meant.

That night after supper, Anna crept into Lizzie!s kitchen to talk. Lizzie could feel her presence as she tidied up the kitchen and, without turning, she asked "Anna, would you like some coffee?" Anna replied she would. While Lizzie got a cup from the pantry, Anna began to speak of her vision.

She saw a great battle far away and it was different from the wars of her youth when the pony soldiers and the People fought. This battle was filled with death and smoky skies and blasts and explosions and the countless firing of guns. Men were caught on thorns and lying in mud,

lifeless. She did not want to alarm Helen Irene about her vision. Lizzie asked why Helen Irene should be alarmed. Anna told her she saw a soldier that looked like Martin running through mud and falling down as the sky was filled with explosions. But it was so smoky that Anna could not see Martin get up or even move after he had fallen. Anna just wanted to tell her daughter what she had seen. But even Anna could not be sure what it meant. Both agreed that nothing would be said to Helen Irene. Martin would come back from the Great War or not. He was too far away for them to do anything. They would wait for news from the front.

CHAPTER 7

THE GREAT BATTLE

In a war that had started with an assassination of the Austrian heir to the royal throne and his wife in 1914 until now more than four year later and tens of millions of soldiers and civilians dead and starving, the end was not in sight. A battle plan that was aggressive was needed and finally one was agreed to by Allied commanders. After four years, the reasons for the war!s beginning and the historic justifications were being lost in the minds of the populace back home despite politicians repeated claims that their country!s involvement was completely righteous. Territory exchanged from battle to battle was measured in meters rather than leagues. Commanders needed to focus on the task before them-how to defeat the enemy in the field. After four years, who could be certain that any victory on a particular day would result in the end of the conflict. For the trooper in the trenches, such thoughts were beyond them. Their thoughts were centered on whether they would survive the day. Would the enemy attack or would they be called upon to leave the protection of their trench to cross no man!s land under fire. Would they ever be finished with this damn war and go home? Did anyone back home know what was going on over here and did they really care? Morale would go up and down, changing like the weather. The good leaders understood what their troops were going through and did their best to talk with each of the soldiers and do whatever it took to lift their morale. The Allies began a campaign that lasted over 100 days in the Summer of 1918. For American troops, the battles of St Mihiel, Argonne, Chateau Therrey would be long remembered. During this campaign, the exploits of Sgt. Alvin York and the legend of the Lost Battalion would be etched in the annals of American Military History. But there in the middle of the Chateu Therrey battle was Corporal Martin Schonebaum. His division was part of the battle that day. Because he was the fastest soldier in his unit he had served as a runner between units. Accurate communication saved lives and a fast runner was sometimes the only way to coordinate an attack. Running seemed somehow safer than sitting in a trench with artillery shells pounding your position. But not this time for Martin. In an exchange of artillery fire, Martin was wounded by a bursting shell that spread shrapnel in a 10 foot radius. His fellow troopers found him buried in mud. While his wounds required a brief stay in the field hospital, he returned to duty, fighting until the end of the campaign. While in the hospital, Martin took the time to write his last letter to Helen Irene before the signing of the Armistice of November 11. He received a Purple Heart for his wounds. He wanted her to know he was OK but he had to tell her he had been wounded because, although he had returned to action, he was still limping and did not know how long that would last.

Dearest Helen Irene,

Please do not worry. I was slightly injured in the explosion of an artillery shell near my position while charging a German fortified position. It blew me into the air and I landed in a muddy hole where my buddies found me face down. They pulled me out of the mud before I drowned. I was very lucky or someone was watching over me from above!

Before I was carried off the field, I witnessed our colors waving over a German position that they had held for over a year. I spent two days in a field hospital, which is simply a large tent several miles behind our lines. I was well treated and released to return to my unit. The explosion did result in a few cuts and some bleeding but I am fully intact but covered in a few bandages. When the corpsman cleaned my wounds, it was the first time some of the mud was washed off me in days.

All of us are needed on the line and I am heading back to my unit as I write. I really feel that we are nearing the end of this conflict. Many German soldiers have surrendered and I could see from the look in their eyes that this is nearly over.

I so look forward to getting home soon and starting our lives together.

With Deepest Love,
Martin

The final 100 days of the war resulted in the collapse of the German Austrian army and the signing of an Armistice on November 11. Celebrations were heard up and down the Allied lines and bells throughout Europe rang for hours. The Great War, the war to end all wars, was over and the troops were headed home! Martin and his fellow soldiers almost did not care what the war was all about. Their focus was on going home and getting on with their lives.

Martin sailed home on Thanksgiving day and arrived in New York on December 10. He carried his Purple Heart in his baggage, awarded because of his wounds. According to his orders he was scheduled to take a train to Chicago, then to Omaha and finally back to Sioux Falls where he would be mustered out. His final train ride would be to Bonesteel where he expected to be arriving by Christmas. Those who processed the troops landing in New York strongly suggested that the arriving soldiers wear their uniforms until they were processed out. It made the transit by train go more smoothly without having to produce copies of their papers.

Still in uniform, Martin dashed to the nearest telegraph office and sent news of his arrival in New York and his expected return to Bonesteel. It cost a great deal of money but it was faster than any letter he could have written at that point. He had wanted to send a flowery message but that was out of the question with a telegram that all of South Dakota would probably read before it reached his parents and Helen Irene. The flowery stuff would have to wait. He had a few hours before his train to Chicago left and he realized he should write the dean of the Law School and advise he wanted to finish his studies and requested a seat in the class graduating in 1919. He dispatched that letter and hoped for the best.

CHAPTER 8

HOME

She spotted him before anyone else. He was walking up Main Street towards Lizzie!s house. Snowflakes were swirling about and the winds were whipping through the air but she knew it just had to be him in the drab greenish brown coat trudging up the road. He had a slight limp in his gait but otherwise looked sound from her standpoint. She screamed to Lizzie and Anna, "He is here!" And after weeks of travel over land, sea and prairie, Martin was home. She knew he would stop and see his parents first before he came to spend some time with Helen Irene. Martin!s parents lived a mile further down the road. Helen picked up the new-fangled telephone and connected with Martin!s father, August, and told him Martin had arrived and was walking towards the farm. Helen Irene said that her father Sam would give Martin a ride, after of course Martin and Helen said their hello!s. August thanked Helen and went to tell his wife the good news. Yes, Martin was finally home, a decorated soldier with his life ahead of him.

Before Martin could open the gate of the picket fence that guarded the Lindley house, Helen Irene flew from the front porch and wrapped her arms around Martin and welcomed him home. They hugged and kissed, not caring that the neighbors could see. Coming home from war was an event. Everyone would understand. The long absence was over. Now they could say intimately what they had only inferred in their letters. Life would begin now. Love would fill their lives. Lizzie walked down the porch steps and embraced Martin. Anna quietly came from behind the house and quietly offered thanks for Martin!s return to Helen Irene. Then Sam came from the barn with his rig all hitched up and Martin hopped in, promising to return after he had spent some time with his parents. Lizzie said: "Martin, please let your parents know you and they are invited to Sunday dinner, after Church. We want to welcome you home properly."

The following Sunday Martin, his father August, his mother Anna Kapleman Schonebaum, his older brother August, Junior (Gus) and his wife Louella who had known Helen Irene since they were children, arrived at Lizzie's for supper. Lizzie greeted them at the front door and was joined in welcoming Martin!s family by Sam, Helen Irene as well as Lizzie!s parents Anna and Charles Marshall. It was a large gathering but everyone was looking forward to the event, not only to welcome Martin back home but to taste the food prepared by Helen Irene, who was known far and wide for her fried chicken and her deserts. She had worked hard with Lizzie!s help to prepare a feast that would be remembered for years. Martin thought as he ate the meal Helen Irene prepared how lucky he was. He had not eaten like this since he left South Dakota almost twenty months before.

During supper, Martin described how his time in France had resulted in his leg wounds. He told all gathered that his unit had been gassed and that he had been slightly injured before he could get his gas mask on. He described the heroism of many of his friends from South Dakota serving with him and how some of them pulled him out of a bomb crater filled with mud and water. He had been rendered unconscious by the blast from a German artillery shell and cut by the shrapnel from the shell. Anna Marshall listened closely to Martin!s story, with eyes wide open looked at Lizzie and just nodded. It had happened as she had seen it months before. He also described how many of his fellow soldiers had died from the 1918 Pandemic that had swept not only the Army but much of Europe. It was sad that so many had perished after surviving the worst war that western civilization had ever endured. No one would ever say they served in vain. They were warriors. They had served and would always be treated with dignity and respect.

After supper and the dishes cleared, Martin stood and took Helen Irene!s hand in his and spoke to everyone in the room. He said that they were sorry to have surprised all with their decision to marry. But with his induction into the Army, everything had occurred so fast that he had not had time to ask properly for permission from Sam and Lizzie to marry Helen Irene. Instantly, Lizzie and Sam in unison said, "You have made Helen Irene and us so happy! You have our permission". Helen Irene said "Martin you have made me so happy and your parents have made me so welcome into your family. I love you so much." She then took over the floor and told all that she and Martin had talked with Father Francis at the Immaculate Conception Catholic Church and set a date for next July for the wedding and they would both return to University after Christmas and earn their degrees, Martins in law and she her Bachelor!s. They planned to settle in Bonesteel but did not know where they would live but they thought they would build a house near town. Then she asked Gus and Louella if they would be Martin!s best man and her maid of honor for the wedding. She hugged them both when they agreed. She then asked Anna to bless her and Martin and their marriage. When Anna was finished, they settled down for coffee and Helen Irene!s pie.

On July 20, 1919 Martin and Helen Irene were wed in the Catholic church in Bonesteel. The local newspaper printed a short story about the wedding:

First Female Graduate of University and
Local War Hero Wed

Childhood sweethearts Helen Irene Lindley and Martin August Schonebaum, a decorated veteran from the Great War we re we d th i s p a s t S a tu rd ay a t Immaculate Conception Catholic Church. Helen Irene was attended by Louella Schonebaum, the sister in law of Martin. Martin!s best man was his brother August Schonebaum. Helen Irene recently graduated with distinction from University and is the first known female graduate therefrom. Martin earned his law degree from the University of South Dakota Law School and will be joining the law firm of Meister and Strood.

After the wedding Martin and Helen Irene went to Chicago for their honeymoon. Although Martin had traveled through Chicago on his return from France, he had not spent any time in the City. He thought of visiting the museums and see the architecture of the skyscrapers that made Chicago one of the most interesting cities in the world. He thought about visiting several auto dealerships to see what would soon be available throughout the country. But Helen Irene had definite ideas of her own. In her last two years at University, she had joined the local chapter of the Suffragette movement. She was appalled that we had fought and won a world war with the help of the "women back home" but women could not vote. Further, countries in Europe were liberalizing voting rights to grant equal status for women. Indeed in the United States, many of the western states were amending the state constitutions to allow women to vote. But she had learned that unless the US Constitution was amended by the Nineteenth Amendment, women could not have the right to vote in every state. She had become an active member of the South Dakota suffragette movement. She remembered meeting the key leaders of the movement when she and her parents had visited Chicago when she was sixteen. Her mother had been active in the movement since. Helen wrote letters, prepared leaflets, drew posters, contacted legislators and marched. Congress, after two years of fighting, had finally approved the amendment and sent it to the states for the necessary approval. South Dakota was one of the early states to consider the amendment. Helen Irene and her family were among the prime movers for the amendment in South Dakota and she wanted to meet with the suffragette leaders in Chicago to discuss strategy. The museums would have to wait. Martin walked Helen Irene from the hotel to the offices of the Illinois chapter of the National Suffragette League. There Helen Irene spent several hours talking strategy and the importance of South Dakota in the effort to pass this critical Amendment. She would return to Bonesteel with a new zeal. She had raised the issue of the vote for Native Americans and particularly Native American women in those meetings. She was disappointed with the response. The movement was built upon a coalition that was gaining momentum and introducing this issue would probably result in a derailment. Somewhat dispirited, she realized that in some states like her own the sentiment against the Native Americans was still strong. What the leaders of the movement were saying was probably true even in states like South Dakota where the pro women's vote had a real chance of success.

South Dakota, Illinois, Michigan and Wisconsin were the first states to ratify the 19th Amendment on December 4, 1919. Through the efforts of women across the country, the amendment became effective in time for the National election in November 1920. Shamefully, some states did not finally ratify the Nineteenth Amendment until after the 1960!s, long after it had become the law of the land. Mississippi became the last to ratify the Amendment in 1984. Helen Irene felt exhilarated to have participated actively in the fight. The legacy of her family to fight for what you believe in had come to the surface and she was proud of that. She had talked about the fight with Anna. Anna could not comprehend the concept of women not having a say in decisions because so many of the indigenous people made their decisions with the approval of women. What was wrong with that she had wondered. But it was good to see that Helen Irene was a fighter like Anna was.

Martin was amazed at how little he had learned in Law School about the practice of law. His first month after graduation he had spent hours learning the practical aspects of his trade. The law firm!s practice was what one today would call a general one. While the transfer of land, whether by sale or transfer a death, made up the bulk of their practice, occasionally some matters became the subject of a dispute that could only be resolved by litigation. Martin sought out this type of practice mostly because this was the one area that the Law School had excelled in and Martin enjoyed a good fight. The fact that he was willing to put on the gloves and "duke it out" made resolving disputes easier. His reputation as a scrapper helped him build his practice. The better he became, the harder he worked and the less time he spent at home.

After they had gotten back from Chicago, they had temporarily moved in with Helen Irene!s parents. The idea of their own home was just a dream, certainly an expensive one. Sam and Lizzie had given up their bedroom and moved downstairs to a bedroom next to the kitchen. It was awkward at times to be living with your in-laws but the house was very well built and sounds did not carry through the house. But one of the surprises of living in that house was Anna. She had continued living outside the house in her hut but seemed to invisibly and silently move throughout the main house at will surprising Helen Irene and Martin at inopportune times. Several times they had long conversations about the

living arrangements but finding land that was available and affordable near town was difficult. Moreover, even with new rights for women envisioned by the Nineteenth Amendment, positions for women were few and far between. Fortunately, the trading post was thriving and Lizzie always needed help. Helen Irene began to do the bookkeeping for the business and enjoyed the solitude in the back of the store away from customers and suppliers. She wished she and Martin were spending more time together but she understood that success would require hard work. Many married couples in town lived with their parents and homes all over town were adding extra rooms and otherwise expanding for that reason. As the only child, Helen Irene felt the responsibility of watching over the health of both her grandmother and her mother. Although Lizzie was amazingly active and by all appearances very healthy, life in South Dakota was always a challenge. Moreover, Anna continued to be an anomaly. She was now over 80 but continued her vigorous walks to the trading post each day and silently arranging the goods and sweeping the floors which constantly were filled with dirt and dust tracked in by customers and the wind through the open front door. So living in Lizzie and Sam!s house was a good arrangement. Though Martin would complain from time to time, he realized that he did not have the time to be working on building his own house even if he could find the land. So the arrangement continued.

Christmas of 1919 was approaching and the blending of three cultures was seen throughout the big house. Martin!s parents had gifted the newlyweds with many decorations that traced their origin in Germany. Many had been handed down to Martin!s father from his parents. But many more had come from Anna Kappleman!s parents and had accompanied them from Germany when they migrated to America. Martin was delighted to see many of the favorite things he had known from Christmas past. They were not big items. One might even consider them like small toys. But seeing them throughout the down stairs just brightened Martin!s mood. Lest you think that the home looked entirely German, remember that few cultures celebrate Christmas like the English. The Lindleys were no exception. All about the house were reminders of Christmas from the manger and carved animals to the hand-made wreath that adorned the front door. Helen Irene's grandmother, Anna added a few hand carved figures that dated back to the days she had roamed the prairies on horseback. Satisfied that all was well with Helen Irene and her new husband and the preparations for Christmas were complete, Anna retreated to her hut. That night her visions continued.

CHAPTER 9

FIRST CHRISTMAS

Oh, I suppose that we all have dreams, whether they happen during the depths of sleep at night or even thoughts during the day, those we might call daydreams. But visions are a whole other thing. Sometimes they are a way to focus on a problem and lead us to a solution. Other times they help us recall the events of the day, allowing us to see our shortcomings or realize a verbal slight was not intentional. Perhaps, we were making more of the words than they were intended. Dreams could give us pause and time to reflect. But some dreams or visions are so real and so clear that they seemed to tell us what will happen, sometimes regardless of what we could do to change it.

They are so deep that the person having the vision may not even realize the details of the dream until long after it is over. Some cultures revere those who seemingly can see into the future. Those that do possess the ability to see must be guarded. Those who cannot see, are ready to dismiss and even persecute those who can. Just as Anna could see Martin lying face down in a crater in France during battle, she could see other things, things that just came to her naturally.

That night the smoke from her fire hung in the hut. Anna closed her eyes and began to dream again. She could see a brave young girl dashing about a field of battle helping wherever she could. Others followed her even though she was small, smaller than those around her.

Her hair blew in the breeze behind her, a cap in her back pocket. Though the battle seemed to rage about her, she was calm and her eyes seemed to see everywhere she and the others were needed. She was far away from home but she seemed at peace. Anna remembered girls like this. She had seen them many years ago at Greasy Grass, that great battle between the Lakota and Custer. Anna knew these girls to be brave and unafraid and she had followed them taking care of the wounded and the children. These girls, women really, were every bit as brave as the warriors that held a bow or a rifle or a scalping knife. They held the tribe together. They were warriors. She and Lizzie had done this many years before. Someone else would do the same.

In the morning when she woke, she thought about her dream, her vision and wondered what it meant. She thought about what this girl had looked like and knew this girl in her dream did not look like any she had remembered from long ago. This was someone different, someone new.

Was this just her imagination at play or was it something else. She did not know. Anna would set the dream aside and let it be for now. She had been working on hand crafted gifts for Helen and that helped her think about the meaning of the vision. Maybe something else would happen that would give better meaning to her dream. Yes, time would reveal something more about this dream. Gradually, she put her dream to action and finished the work on her Christmas gifts.

Christmas was a joyous holiday in Bonesteel. The small Catholic community would celebrate the birth of the Christ child together at midnight Mass at the Immaculate Conception. At church the parishioners would listen to the Latin prayers and the Gospel and the sermons and flock around the elaborate Manger scene. Helen Irene thought the baby figurine looked precious in the manger and thought, about the baby: maybe, someday. Yes someday, like Mary and Joseph, she and Martin would have a little one of their own. But now they were so busy and for now it seemed so far away that she put the thought out of her mind.

Anna, who had come to Mass with Charles, Lizzie and Sam sat in the back pew, staring at Helen Irene and thought again about her dream.

They returned to the house and began the Christmas celebration by exchanging a few gifts. Martin gave Helen Irene a beautiful Christmas broach that he had purchased in Chicago while on their honeymoon. Helen cherished the broach and kept it throughout her life as a memory of that first Christmas. Martin was not a vain person; in fact he was a very humble and kind person. But Helen always noticed how carefully Martin kept his hair. He had let it grow out since the war but always kept it neat and in place. She thought maybe he was a little too proud of his strawberry blonde hair but she loved him for that. Helen had found what she wanted in the catalogue at the trading post and special ordered a matching brush and comb, each monographed with his initials. Martin loved his gift and was reminded how thoroughly Helen Irene knew him. Anna gave Helen Irene a pair of hand-made moccasins that were fur lined.

But she also gave her something else. It was a pair of miniature moccasins hand stitched and beaded. Everyone thought they were so adorable and said so. But Helen Irene gave Anna a peculiar look for a few seconds and then gave her a warm hug and a kiss, thanking her for both gifts. Martin seemed not to understand what had just happened.

The next morning, the women were up early beginning the preparations for Christmas dinner. Charles had driven over from the trading post and he and Martin and Sam began the day cutting wood, gathering eggs for breakfast, milking the cows and selecting the right hen for dinner. It was a good way to start the day and made breakfast that much more enjoyable, knowing that they had accomplished something already. After breakfast they completed the chores and used the sharpened ax on the biggest hen in the yard. Martin brought the plucked hen to the kitchen and handed it off to Helen Irene, made sure she had enough wood for the stove and got cleaned up before retiring to the Living Room. The embers from the Christmas Eve fire in the hearth were fed with proper amounts of kindling and wood until a crackling fire was going, warming the entire downstairs. These would be the Christmas memories all present would carry throughout the rest of their lives. Truly, if anyone would ever ask them to recall a memory of Christmas, each would say pretty much the same: family, a warm fire, a freshly cut fir tree, Christmas decorations adorning the room, the aroma of freshly brewed coffee and the incredibly good food being prepared for Christmas dinner. But the most important memory of all would be family. For Martin and Helen Irene this first Christmas seemed like it would be the best they would have. But that would not be true. They would be memories just the same.

CHAPTER 10

THE MOCCASINS

Christmas was past and the longest and coldest Winter had set in blanketing Bonesteel and indeed the whole of South Dakota in a deep freeze. Some days the high temperature was zero degrees. The idea of wind chill had not been conceived yet so there was really no way of telling how cold it felt. But the good thing about the bitter cold, it was almost too cold to snow. The farm animals were kept in the barn at night but it was still important to muck out the floor of the barn if life was to survive in the confines of the barn. Life would go on, the chores would be there every day. Vacations from the routine just were not heard of. But winter had its pluses and minuses. The crisp air in the morning and the aroma of a cup of coffee were great ways to start the day. But in the winter when daylight would come much later, the household would still rise before five A.M. each day. Chores would be undertaken by kerosene lit lamps. The cold seemed to keep the odor of the animal waste closer to the ground floor making that task more tolerable. Each morning when Martin went out to the barn, he checked the hut to see if Anna was up. She usually was and had made her trip to the privy her first task of the day before she would trudge into the kitchen for her morning cup of coffee. This morning she was up, bundled in her buffalo robe and staring at the morning stars. Yes she was thinking, the time was close at hand. The family would change and she hoped that she would see that change come to pass. She nodded to Martin as he walked to the barn while she went into the kitchen to see if the coffee was ready to drink. Martin wondered what she was doing.

Later that morning the air moistened and warmed up a bit and then the sky changed from a brilliant sunshine to dark grey and then to almost black with the winds beginning to howl. A storm was coming and it would be bad. The family hustled about rounding the animals to the barn and locking down what was not. Lizzie rushed to the trading post and made sure that all the shutters were barred. A sign that she kept inside for such occasions was tacked to the door indicating that the store was closed due to the storm. Anna, who had already arrived at the store had seen the weather change while waiting for Lizzie, helped secure everything before she climbed into the buggy. They made it home as the storm began.

It proved to be the worst storm of the 20th Century so far. Two and a half feet of snowfall but with winds blowing steady at 40 miles an hour with gusts up to 60, whole houses were covered completely by drifts. People and animals simply disappeared from sight for days. No one ventured far from their homes. Roads were untraveled. The well prepared emerged unscathed. Many were not prepared at all. During daylight unless the lamps or candles were alit, it was just plain dark throughout the house. Ropes were stretched from the house to the privy and to the barn lest folks simply wandered off into the storm. Some that did were found a month later, still frozen in place.

It was during this storm, dubbed the Blizzard of 1920, that Martin and Helen Irene spent nearly all of three days in the warm confines of the master bedroom, laughing, talking about life and the future and making love. Oh they came up at times for air, for food and information about the storm, but returned quickly to the warmth of the master bedroom. The nervousness of the honeymoon was over and the tensions and stress of the past few months of adjusting to married life disappeared. Now the intimacy of two practiced lovers was evident. Nothing was rushed or hurried. Love and joy tenderness and whispers filled the room. Nothing was planned but they knew that tomorrow would change forever.

Lizzie had insisted that Anna move into the house when they had arrived home from the trading post. This storm will be too cold and too strong to stay in Anna!s hut. So for the next three nights Anna stayed in the room next to the master bedroom. Every movement in the bed in the next room could be heard and the whispers that Martin and Helen Irene shared sounded quite clear to Anna. Yes, at times the house shook, maybe from the wind and maybe not. Nothing would be the same after the storm. She closed her eyes and smiled. It would be weeks from then before she knew that they would have a child on the way but that night she felt a spirit stirring in her soul.

It was quiet outside now. The wind had stopped or at least so much snow was caked against the house that she could not hear anything. Helen looked over at the chest of drawers that stood at the foot of their bed. Reflected in the mirror over that chest were the two tiny moccasins that Anna had given her at Christmas. Anna had foreseen all this. Nothing that Anna ever did really surprised Helen Irene. She was quite a significant figure in her life. The older Helen Irene got, the more she resembled her grandmother, the dark features, the black hair which Helen Irene always wore short. She knew she was as tall as she ever would be which was shorter than most and quite a bit shorter than Lizzie. Like Anna her eyes could instantly turn from penetrating to warmth. It was as if she was cutting into you one second and caressing your heart the next.

When very young she would listen intently to Anna!s stories about she and Lizzie leaving home and traveling the prairies with Sitting Bull and the rest of the Teton Sioux. How she had envied her mother but she knew she could never do what Anna had done. She could not leave her husband behind as Anna had done. Martin was part of her and no matter what now that he had come back to her from the war, she knew they would be together, inseparable until her last breath. But maybe the child that was intended to have those little moccasins would take a great adventure, travel far and help in a great conflict some day. The moccasins, the moccasins, how could Anna have predicted so well?

CHAPTER 11

THE VOTE

It had been an enormous push to get the Nineteenth Amendment in place for adoption before the Presidential election of 1920. The right to vote for women was an interesting struggle that had many reversals and small victories. When Independence was declared in 1776, women had the right to vote in several of the Colonies. But when the Constitution was adopted, only white males had the right to vote and the former Colonies, then states, amended their laws to eliminate the right to vote for women. By the 1840's the Suffragette movement began to exercise its muscle and states were gradually being convinced to consider allowing women the right to vote. As new states became part of America, they almost universally granted voting rights to the women in their state. But it was easy to backtrack on the grant of these rights without constitutional protection. For example, the territory of Utah granted voting rights when it was formed but reversed its position when the territory became a state. Later it granted voting rights in 1907. There seemed to be no permanence without an amendment to the Constitution. The resistance to granting voting rights was influenced by the belief that women should mind their own business, stay at home, raise the children, manage the household and be subservient to their spouses. This was evident even when one of the early attempts to pass an amendment to the US Constitution in 1888. That amendment would only grant voting rights to women who were beyond childbearing age and to widows as long as they owned property. Obviously that was an amendment without meaning and went down to defeat.

The real problem with amending the US Constitution was that it had high hurdles to overcome in order to be effective. The founders believed that the Constitution was to be an enduring document but changes to it should require an overwhelming agreement among the people and the states that made up the US. To amend it, the Constitution requires, in the absence of a Constitutional Convention called for by two-thirds of the states, an amendment approved by two thirds of the Senate and two- thirds by the House of Representatives AND then approval by three fourths of the legislatures of the states then admitted to the United States. The Suffragettes tactics were to first convince a number of states to themselves grant the right to vote and then with a base in hand to lobby Congress to approve an amendment. By the time that the United States entered the Great War, only the states of Montana, Nevada, Utah, New York, Arizona, Kansas, Oregon, California, Washington, Idaho and Colorado granted women the right to vote. But by supporting the federal government's efforts during the Great War, through support for the Red Cross and other organizations that helped our armed forces, as well as support for raising government bonds to pay for the war, political favors were earned. By the end of the War, Michigan, Oklahoma, Georgia Minnesota and South Dakota had joined those states granting voting rights to women. It was through the efforts of many of the important families in South Dakota that these rights were on the verge of being won. The Marshall, the Lindley and the Schonebaum families lent their political influence to this cause. The women in these families such as Lizzie and Helen Irene were no longer going to be treated as second class citizens and pushed for change.

But in South Dakota, persistence counted. Six times efforts to pass voting rights for women were proposed and defeated in the legislature. In 1919, the seventh attempt was approved. Politicians resisting feared the potential political clout of women and that made change come slowly. Women in the movement understood that simply having the state legislature grant the right to vote was not enough. They had seen that legislative bodies could easily take away the hard fought right and felt that a federal amendment was still a must even though the hurdle was high. But Helen and Lizzie and countless other women across the country were persistent and determined. They were not bashful and were vocal. If they needed to march or carry signs they would do it. Change had to come.

Finally President Wilson backed an amendment which became the Nineteenth Amendment and in 1919, both Houses of Congress had approved it by the requisite two thirds vote and the amendment was submitted to the state governors to have their legislatures approve the amendment. Neither the effort to get states to approve the right to vote or convince the state legislatures to approve the Nineteenth Amendment was achieved by the proponents wishing that legislators would do the right thing or just talking seductively or batting eyes. In many cases it took raw political pressure which women of significance like the Schonebaums, the Lindleys and the Marshalls were willing to apply. Financially supporting candidates that would seek approval if elected was the one sure way to influence the approval process. In short order South Dakota, and thirteen other states had voted to ratify the amendment. By June of 1920, thirty-five of the necessary 36 states necessary to ratify had done so. Tennessee took up the amendment in August 1920 with the Tennessee Senate approving on August 12 and the House approving by one vote on August 18. This assured that women could vote in the 1920 Presidential election. When Helen Irene read the paper August 19, she knew that the child she was carrying, if a girl, would have the right to vote when she reached proper age and that so would Helen Irene. She rushed around the kitchen shouting for joy telling her husband Martin, "we did it, we did it. We have the right to vote!"

CHAPTER 12

CANAWAPE KASNA WI

The air was crisp and the mist hung over the range. But the sky was bright and clear as the moon was full. A pale pink color gave the moon an eerie look as the moon lit the sky obscuring even the brightest stars. Anna Marshall squatted at the front door of her sod hut and listened. She knew that it was time for Helen Irene to give birth. Everything that she knew from the sky and the many times that she had given birth to her sons and Lizzie told her that tonight would be the night. She did not need the moon to tell her but it did. But it told her much more. It had whispered that a warrior would be born tonight. Everything was aligned. She would live to see it and she was glad.

She had seen the arrival of Helen Irene's doctor, Doc Schreiber that morning to check on Helen Irene. He had left Lizzie's home earlier in the day to make his other house calls. It was then not time for the birth. It would be tonight she knew. The moon told her so.

She had seen some of her Lakota relatives the week before and told them of the signs she had seen and had told them of the coming of her great grandchild. They would tell others. It was the way the Lakota did things. Although it had been many years since she had visited the reservation at Pine Ridge, she knew how the word of her vision would spread among her relations.

Anna had not only lived to see her daughter Lizzie grow into a beautiful woman but had witnessed the birth of Lizzie!s daughter Helen Irene Lindley. Helen Irene was now ready to give birth and Anna!s heart jumped for joy at the prospect of the arrival of a new warrior, her great grandchild. It would be a good thing. Life would carry on. Anna could rest in peace. Her clan would continue. But they should be here too.

It was nearly 10 o!clock but in this part of the country the sun set early this time of the year. It was the second week of October and all across the state, the farms had already harvested the grasses and crops.

The farmers knew that the growing season was finished and the first killer frost was days away. It was the first full growing season since the end of the Great War in Europe and the sons that had seen the world had returned and had helped with the harvest. These sons had experienced the cold of the trenches and knew from their seasons before the War how cold it could get in South Dakota. And with the colder temperatures would come the fierce winds from the mountains north and west. When those winds came, nothing that grew would withstand the wind and cold. The first reminder of the fierce winds to come had swept in earlier that day and had swept the fields of any residue of hay the farmers had harvested. The dirt roads were covered with remnants from the fields.

The divots from the wagons and buggies and the few cars that traveled through this part of the state were neatly filled in with cut grasses from the fields making the roads seem to disappear even in the light of the full moon. This moon for the farmers was the Harvest Moon which announced to all that the harvest was at the end. For the rest of the populace it was an Indian Moon. For Anna it was "Canwape Kasna Wi", meaning the moon of the "Wind that Shakes the Leaves". The winds and the cold would come soon. The Lakota living in poverty on the Pine Ridge reservation abutting these farms, too had gathered their meager crops but through traditions knew this to be a favorable time to hunt. The brightly lit sky would make the night creatures stand out and easier to kill. For some of the tribe, the success of the hunts would allow some to survive the winter. But the creatures of the night were smart enough to move from the reservation to the adjacent farm lands and now the roads covered with cut grasses There they were able to feed on the grasses not completely harvested by the farmers and avoid the hunting parties from the reservation. Of course the tribe never had agreed to these artificial boundaries that defined the reservation and simply followed the game wherever they were. Fights would start and guns were fired in the night, sometimes at the Lakota and sometimes at the white farmers. But that was life in the middle of South Dakota at the end of 1920. Life was harsh. Survival was harsher.

William Red Bear and his brother Martin, of the Redbear clan of the Lakota had borrowed a used car and driven from the Pine Ridge Reservation to Bonesteel. They had heard Anna's predictions about a birth of her great grandchild and planned to visit with Anna to learn more. They had heard that tonight was the predicted birth night and had brought a gift, a birth feather to commemorate the event.

Dr. Schreiber was making his appointed rounds that night, stopping here for one sick household and there for another. Doc had significantly upgraded his practice with a crank telephone and a used Model T Ford. His time in making the usual rounds was cut in half but the new-fangled phone meant he was getting calls at all hours of the night. Doc!s wife had taken a call from the Schonebaum house while he was on the road. Doc was back on the road to check in with Helen Irene who, according to the message his wife took, was feeling severe pains in her abdomen. This was going to be a difficult birth because Helen!s grandmother Anna was living with them and planned to perform a Lakota ceremony at the birth.He knew from his past encounters with this woman, that modern medicine and the old ways did not mix well. But of greater concern was that the baby was not in the normal position for the birth. It could get tricky.

The Schonebaum homestead was near Bonesteel South Dakota and was in the heart of farm country. It was located only a 100 miles from the Pine Ridge Reservation. While Anna had never lived on the reservation, her clan did. She had been happy with her husband and he had never been regretful that they had married even though his white neighbors shunned him for marrying this "thing". The white community held strong anti Indian feelings and were of the opinion that South Dakota belonged to the white race and the treaties with the tribes be damned. While Anna!s daughter Lizzie did not feel this way, nor did Lizzie!s daughter Helen Irene, Lizzie!s husband!s family did. Anna knew she must show her future great grandchild the right path to follow even in a white world. After her husband!s death, Anna had returned more and more to the ceremonies she learned from her ancestors. She would never abandon her granddaughter Helen Irene, nor any of her children. Now living in the sod hut behind Helen Irene and her husband Martin!s house, she intended to make sure the great Spirit would watch over the birth of her great grandchild. She respected Martin and Helen!s decision to have Doc deliver the child. But the warrior spirit had to embrace this new born child. Only she could do that.

CHAPTER 13

DOC'S MAGIC

Martin greeted Doc at the front door. Doc noted that Martin seemed quite calm considering this was the birth of his first child. While he did not know Martin as well as he knew his wife Helen, he remembered that Martin had returned from the Great War and was a decorated soldier.

He had heard from his wife that Helen and Martin had grown up in Bonesteel as childhood sweethearts and had graduated from the University of South Dakota. He also knew that Martin was practicing law in town. So Doc felt he understood why Martin, as a wounded veteran, was so calm. "Helen Irene is upstairs with Lizzie and Anna," he said. Doc hung up his coat and took his medical bag upstairs to find Helen thrashing about in the big bedroom at the top of the stairs. Lizzie thanked Doc for returning so soon and reminded him that Helen had been born very quickly after Lizzie had gone into labor. Maybe quick births ran in the family. She hoped that Dr. Strauss had made a note in the files before he retired. Most of Dr. Strauss's patients had moved to Doc's practice when the former retired. Doc quickly got to work and after examining her realized immediately that Helen Irene, though having contractions would not give birth soon. It might not be as easy as her mother's birth.

Anna had heard Doc's car arrive and went into the house and up to Helen Irene's room and sat in the corner where she would watch. Doc had noticed Anna sitting in the corner as soon as he had walked into the room. Anna who he had anticipated to be an issue was quietly sitting in a chair near the window looking away from the bed but seeing everything.

After he had finished his preliminary exam, Helen suddenly awoke in pain and cried out. She saw Doc and asked, "How much longer is this pain going to last?" Before Doc could answer, Anna spoke, "until the dawn. The baby will be here at dawn." Doc had thought it might be earlier but just nodded, thinking she could be right. He also thought it could be much longer if the position of the baby was not correct. He saw that the women were keeping Helen Irene in as much comfort as possible and then went down stairs.

Doc had dealt with hundreds of births, deaths and serious injuries since he came to Bonesteel. Now that he had a used car, he had expanded his practice. It had not really made him a wealthy man but he was satisfied he was taking care of as many in the community as he could. Maybe one of the children he delivered would someday become a physician and do the same for the people he had been doing. He nodded to Martin and sat down. He was glad that he had gotten the call to come to the Schonebaum's even if he would have to wait a while before the delivery. Doc thought about the retired Dr. Strauss who had moved to the big city of Omaha south of Bonesteel along the Missouri. Dr. Strauss had delivered both Martin and Helen Irene. Maybe he would drop a letter to Dr. Strauss announcing the birth of their first child. But he was getting ahead of the event.

After about an hour sitting almost in complete silence, he heard a scream from upstairs and shouts from Anna and Lizzie to come back to the room. Doc bounded up the stairs, took note of where his medical bag was and rushed to Helen Irene's side. She was screaming that something was wrong. When he had seen Helen Irene earlier in the day he was bothered by the position of the baby then but felt it would resolve itself as the birth got closer. When he had arrived that evening, his examination did not confirm or dismiss a problem. But this time he noted that the baby seemed to have stopped moving completely and was clearly not in the right position. This was going to be difficult. Helen was right. There was a problem. Although Helen Irene was a small woman, by all measures the baby would be small. But he would have to act quickly and could not count on the baby naturally coming to the right position. This had never happened to him before but he had studied it in school. He quickly began kneading her lower belly and making sure that she slowed down her pushing. While he was as gentle as he could be, it did not make the pain go away or Helen Irene!s screaming subside. Suddenly, the baby slid into position and everything was as natural as could be. An hour later, just at dawn, the baby arrived! A healthy baby girl! Just as the baby was wrapped up in a towel, Lizzie was shouting down to Martin that he was a father and that Helen Irene was the mother of a beautiful baby girl. The first thing that Helen Irene said was "Anna hand me the moccasins for the baby." Before Martin could get upstairs, the women had agreed that this precious little girl would be named Helen Elizabeth, after her mother and grandmother.

Everyone congratulated Doc for his quick skill. Martin found a cigar of Sam's in the desk and gave it to Doc while patting him on the back. Martin insisted on paying the full bill in cash. Martin did not believe in being in debt and quickly settled the account. Doc said good night after he made a final check on Helen Irene and the baby. He thought, well probably not a future doctor this time but he had hopes for the next.

As Doc was leaving, he saw two large shadows on the front porch of Lizzie!s house. Sitting in the dark in two rocking chairs were Martin and William Redbear. They told Doc they were there to meet the warrior who was being born tonight. Doc went back in the house and told Martin he had two guests outside on the porch. Martin went out and introduced himself and found out these men, Martin and William Redbear, were relatives of Anna and had come to see the new born warrior. "Warrior?"

Martin inquired. "Yes", Martin said, "Anna had been telling the tribe that her granddaughter was going to give birth to continue the Sitting Bull line" She had said that the child would be a "warrior". Martin welcomed them and invited them into the house and called up to Anna to tell her she had visitors. William and Martin Redbear were greeted by Anna holding the baby and were pleased to meet the little girl, Helen Elizabeth. They offered the baby their blessings of peace and love and left a birth feather with Anna. Then they departed. Anna gave the feather to Helen Irene for safe keeping.

While Martin adored being a father and instantly fell in love with this tiny girl, he made it clear to all that he was not going to be called dad or father or papa or pop by Helen Elizabeth. He insisted that his children would address him as Martin. That was how they could best express their love and respect. After all everyone addressed Lizzie by her name and Anna too. Why couldn't that apply to him. The women teased him a bit and Lizzzie said, "are you concerned about people thinking you are old if your daughter walked around calling you 'Father'. But with her name being Helen Elizabeth, there might be some confusion with two Helen's in the house. What should we call this bright and shining light with the beaming face and curly dark hair? She looks just like her mother and a lot like Anna". Helen Irene wanted to address her after her own mother and began to call her "Elizabeth". Martin began to call her "little Helen". He held her in his arms and said, "Just look at 'little Helen', she is so sweet and precious." The women objected saying it would confuse everyone if we started calling her that. Martin responded, "Little children spend the first few years reaching for their mother with open arms calling 'Mama, Mother or Mom or even Ma.' The child will know what she wants to call her mother". The women remembered that conversation well and repeated it throughout the years. For that was the day that Helen Irene became "Ma" and the baby girl called, 'Helen'. She was not Midge yet. That would come later. What was clear though was that he would be called "Martin".

CHAPTER 14

MA IT IS

Helen grew quickly and enjoyed being the first born in a family dominated by strong women. It was a family that was a strong proponent of education and particularly the education of women and that started early in life, knowing current affairs, understanding numbers and figures, history and literature. It started with baby steps, coupled with an inquisitive mind and an adventuresome spirit. Helen wanted to know the why and how of things and what would come next. Books, large and small, would dominate her whole life. They were an escape to another world and a source of knowledge. But Martin and Helen Irene!s earliest memory of Helen!s voracious appetite for learning was with the daily newspaper. It began with Helen bolting down the steps of the front porch to gather in the morning newspaper for her parents. By the time she was three or four years of age, she would read it front to back before her parents sat down for breakfast and proceed to talk about the events reported in the news over her breakfast.

Of course she learned all the necessary things that a growing young women raised in the country would learn but being the first born meant that obligations usually reserved for boys were also experienced. Leading, taking risks, being outspoken and free to express her views and opinions with confidence were traits that were ingrained at an early age. By the time she was approaching four years of age, her mother gave birth to Helen!s brother Robert who was always known as Bob. Both Martin and Helen Irene were initially concerned about how Helen would react to sharing the roost with a sibling. But Helen surprised her parents because she demonstrated early her maternal instincts without a hint of jealousy. Her interests in learning and knowledge naturally transformed to teaching the newborn all that she could. Much was just her nature, a lot was intentional but some was just unintended. For instance, just as Martin had predicted, Helen, from the day she could talk, called Helen Irene, "Ma". Of course many in that part of the country referred to their parents as their Pa and Ma. But even from the days of her first words, her parents were Martin and Ma. It was not just who Helen Irene was, her mother, but in Helen!s mind, it was her mother!s name. It was never meant to be demeaning or belittling. It was a name of endearment and love and Helen Irene accepted it as such. Helen Irene was then and always, "Ma". Her younger brother Bob, born two years later, picked this up watching and listening to Helen when learning his first words.

Bob was a good natured baby but was a giant compared to Helen!s stature. Ma knew from her pregnancy that this baby was going to be really large. By the time he was three, he was nearly as tall as Helen and growing like a corn stalk. With his dark features and dark hair, he was already a handsome boy and like his father seemed to take a great interest in how his hair looked. He idolized his older sister and followed her wherever she went. It did not seem unusual, when Bob was very young, to see a "big" sister leading her younger brother back and forth around the farm. It became a source of parental amusement though to see in later years their tiny daughter leading around her younger, but taller, brother around, sometimes by the hand and mostly not.

One of their favorite activities as children was playing cowboys and Indians. Helen always wanted to be the Indian and she carried a pouch as she bounded over the hills with Bob chasing her. Her mother's horse Bella was long gone but she and Bob rode their uncle Gus's horses,

Cinnamon and Spice, as part of their war games. Though she never opened her pouch as part of the games, she knew that the precious contents, the moccasins, were with her throughout the wars. The other game that they played from time to time was the recreation of the great battles of the Great War. For this they used the furrows of the newly plowed fields on the farm. Bob and Helen would both be on the same team fighting the imaginary German army hiding in the next furrow. After the game, Helen and Bob would earn medals fashioned from the caps of pop bottles and rewarded with cookies baked by Ma. Martin would watch from the front porch but say nothing about the recreated battles. As she sat down at the kitchen table, Helen wondered if she would ever be the warrior her great grandmother thought she would become.

The school system in Bonesteel was good because it had attracted excellent teachers. Teaching of what we would call today elementary students, were typically done in one room schools. It had been so in Martin and Helen's youth. Nothing much had changed. In the Bonesteel primary school, Mrs. Lawrence taught everything to multiple age children. Helen, who was already beginning fourth grade when Bob joined her for his first day of school, was allowed to learn subjects well above her peers.

So when Bob showed up for his first day of primary school, he had heard much of what Mrs. Lawrence would teach him. Both children excelled with their learning.

While formal learning was something that both children excelled in, what fascinated Helen and eventually her brother was the world beyond Bonesteel. Helen peppered Martin with stories about the Great War, why it happened and why he had gone to a war so far away. Where did he go and what did he see. Had he seen Paris and the Eifel Tower and Notre Dame? What were the French people like? How had he been wounded and who took care of him when he was recovering behind the front. She asked Ma how she had endured Martin!s absence and the fears that he might not come back or might be so injured that it might change him permanently. Helen wanted to know about the biggest city in the Midwest, Chicago, where her parents had honeymooned and New York where he father had arrived home from France. The adventures of her parents seemed so exciting to her. Maybe someday.

CHAPTER 15

THE JUDGE AND HIS BRIDE

The twenties were unlike the pre-war years. The economy was booming, the morals in many places were deteriorating, the explosion of the population, the fundamentalism in religion and the impact of the franchise held by women and the temperance movement all converged by the end of the decade. The temperance movement culminated in Prohibition in 1920. The economic growth had led to over speculation and greed by those that the little guy had trusted with his savings and investments. Little or no regulation allowed businesses to do whatever they wanted. Workers had little protection and were wholly dependent upon the whims of business owners. Despite all that, prosperity seemed as if it would never end and the underlying problems that existed were swept under the rug.

But throughout the 1920!s Martin!s law practice prospered. He had become a partner after five years and was an experienced general practitioner with good litigation skills. He was sought after because he was trustworthy and never seemed to get rattled. The clients were satisfied and let their friends know about it. Things were changing in the Schonebaum!s lives. First, Charles passed away midway through the decade marking the end of a Pioneer era as the newspapers said marking his death. As one of the early settlers in the Bonesteel community, his little trading post fed and clothed the entire community and became the cornerstone for future growth. It was the risk takers that pushed the country to growth and Charles had played his role with great success.

His marriage to Anna Brazos bridged the gap between the Sioux and white settlers although it would be years before a better understanding of the relationship became widespread. At the funeral service, the then 90 year old Anna stood near the graveside surrounded by her sons and three generations of women, Lizzie, Ma and Helen. So much had changed since she and Charles had settled here. She could see him before her dressed in the furs he had trapped telling her that he could provide for her and her children if they wed. He had done that and more. After the priest said his final words over the grave, Anna looked up to the sky and said goodbye.

Anna grieved in her own way but she remained as strong as ever. Although she had moved into the house at Lizzie!s insistence after Helen was born, the family had maintained and preserved the small hut behind the house. Anna would visit it from time to time to reminisce and dream.

One day, Helen wondered where her Great Grandmother was, and found her in the hut staring at the open door in permanent sleep. An era had ended. Word had spread among the Sioux and a contingent of her relatives from the Pine Ridge Reservation came to the interment. Father Francis offered prayers of a Catholic burial and then a member of the tribe, who many understood to be a grand nephew of Sitting Bull, spoke a few words in English and Lakota and Anna was laid to rest. She had lived to see the end of the Civil War, the end of a way of life for her Sioux brethren, end of the fur trade as a way of life, the settlement of South Dakota by immigrants from Europe, the continuation of the emigration from the East, statehood for South Dakota, countrymen marching off to the Great War and fewer returning, the right to vote for women, the birth of her warrior great granddaughter and finally in 1924 the right to vote for Native Americans born in the United States. Much had happened in that space of time and she bore witness to it all. Anna was laid to rest next to her husband of 65 years. After the interment, Helen asked Ma who the Sioux was who spoke at the funeral. Ma replied, "That was Martin Redbear. He and his brother and William live on the reservation and are our relatives, cousins of your great grandmother Anna. They visited us when you were born and gave me a birth feather commemorating your birth. That night Ma told Helen the story about Lizzie and Anna going off to war. Ma told her how Anna felt that Helen would someday be a warrior just as she was. The memory of that conversation brought comfort to Helen whenever she thought of the death of her great grandmother.

Lizzie and Ma ran the trading post for a few years more until they sold it to a newcomer to town. They had agreed to stay for a few months to help with the transition and were glad when that was all over. Lizzie and Sam had deeded their house to Ma and Martin and Sam and Martin had worked over a year to complete an expansion to the house to accommodate the growing family. When completed, Lizzie and Sam reclaimed the old master bedroom and Martin and Ma and the kids moved into the expanded wing of the house. A garage was deemed a necessity and they built one that allowed a covered entrance directly into the house. The car no longer smelled like barn animals. Electricity was brought to the house as the City had completed the lighting of the entire downtown. And then the most wonderful improvement of all was a real bathroom with plumbing to an outdoor cistern. How modern could you get?

Helen shunned playing with dolls, though she treasured the ones her father bought for her. But she still liked to climb over furrows in the plowed fields, pretending she was leading a military charge in France.

Bob still played from time to time but he enjoyed, far more, pretending be the doctor to the wounded. As part of their game, Helen pretended to be wounded in the head when she did not keep her head down. During the long hours of Winter, they enjoyed card games. These mainly consisted of euchre, pitch, rummy, hearts, and eventually bridge with Helen and Bob playing the role of clueless partners to epic battles between Martin and Ma. It was all in fun and the peals of laughter from Ma when Martin would storm off after losing would be talked about for years. Perhaps during these card games was when Helen perfected her laughter. When something struck her as outrageously funny, she would immediately bust out in a laugh so loud, the family was glad the windows were shut. And that laugh would almost never be a short burst; it would last for a long time. She had a good sense of humor and could as easily laugh at herself for something she did that was funny. Her sense of humor was never at the expense of anyone else.

As the new decade began, the country abruptly collapsed as the problems that lay beneath the surface of the economy were laid bare not only by the stock market crash but the risk taking and speculation that had overtaken even the hard working folks. The better part of the country was in the middle of a prolonged drought that affected South Dakota as much as anywhere. Water was scarce and farmers suffered. Martin!s law practice began to falter as few could afford to pay for legal services except with promises and farm animals. One of the local politicians had suggested to Martin that he seek appointment to the bench as a county judge. He talked it over with Ma and they agreed that it was a good idea but would require a lot of belt tightening. So on January 20, 1933, the Honorable Martin A. Schonebaum was sworn in as a County Judge where he presided over civil and criminal matters. He sometimes took Helen to the courtroom to watch some of the proceedings and help carry his papers. Martin was pleased with his decision to serve on the bench. His one regret was that Sam had passed away a few years before he was sworn in. Sam had been one of his biggest advocates over the years and had opened many doors that assisted his practice. Unfortunately, the term of the judicial position was for two years and there was no chance that he could successfully be reelected. This was because the court system in South Dakota was being reduced in size and several of the judges from the appellate courts had agreed to take assignments as County Judges, greatly reducing the chances of reelection against longer-termed judges. He considered his options. Like many younger veterans of his generation, he had borrowed to build the addition to Lizzie!s old home. Now values were falling, banks were looking for opportunities to improve their portfolios and the prospects of a steady stream of income suddenly appearing were slim. A cousin in Council Bluff, Iowa contacted him and alerted him to a position with the Federal Government in Omaha. They were looking for candidates with a law degree or an accounting background to become Treasury Agents. Martin had traveled a few times to Omaha, among those trips, the train ride to boot camp. Ma had never been but had heard great things about the river town. Helen said that she had done some reading on the subject and said it would be a great place to live. After his interview with one of the Treasury agents in Omaha, he was convinced that he would not get the position. But when he returned home, he had received a telegram indicating he had the position if he accepted by return telegram. He did exactly that. Martin and Ma offered Lizzie!s old house up for sale, clearing the loan plus a little surplus, bundled Lizzie, Helen and Bob in the car with a few possessions to follow and set out for Omaha.

CHAPTER 16

A NEW HOME

Compared with Bonesteel, Omaha was a thriving metropolis. Even during the depression, the city was surviving. The meatpacking business, one of the mainstays of Omaha!s economy did quite well. Americans did change their diet in response to the downturn, but people were still eating meat even if only a few times a month. Commerce flowed up and down the Missouri and Omaha was a key juncture between the agriculture belt to the North and West of Omaha but was located on the key east west rail line connecting the West Coast and the East Coast. While not economically immune from the depression, Omaha was in some kind of favorable bubble.

Martin and Ma with the entire clan drove around town and found an ideal location near a Catholic Church, a glorious public park, a fairly new High School and a good elementary school. The home was a two story house that resembled one in picture cards set in Alpine Germany. It had a garage, a basement and two bedrooms on the first floor and two large rooms on the second. Every home in the neighborhood were connected to the public sewer system and had indoor plumbing for bathrooms. This house had a bathroom on each floor. The cost would be a stretch but Ma had set her bonnet on that house on Erskine Street. She would not let Martin dissuade her on this decision. The bonus was the grounds on which the house sat which were large enough to have a fine vegetable garden and fruit trees and room for Helen and Bob to roll through the grass. With the surplus from Lizzie!s house and the security of a federal position with the Treasury Department, the Bank, perhaps to curry favor with the IRS, made a small loan to this young attorney from South Dakota only in Omaha for one day. They moved in the next day, Martin and Ma taking the master bedroom and Helen taking the bedroom on the first floor with Bob taking one and Lizzie the other on the second floor. This move was done with military precision and Helen was watching every move and the decisiveness of each. The next stop was to the schools. Helen would join the Benson High School midyear and would take a brief placement exam to assure the faculty she was accomplished enough to jump right into the second year class. Bob would start in the Catholic elementary school for the remainder of the school year and, if he chose, follow Helen to Benson. By the time they got back from the school adventures, they found Lizzie in the back yard digging the bed for a garden.

From the first day of high school, Helen just soaked in the atmosphere. It was a great learning environment. Here she could sample foreign languages, other than German, which Martin!s mother spoke most of the time. Because she had besieged Martin for tales of France and the Great War, she elected to take as many courses in French as she could. By the time she finished High School, she felt comfortable speaking and writing French but she knew intuitively that she sounded like a South Dakotan with a Nebraskan accent speaking French words. She knew that one of the key disciplines that she would require of any college was its language program. As her senior in High School began, Helen chose Duchene College which was a private girls Catholic school in Omaha. Not only did many of the religious teaching there have European backgrounds with strong in foreign language skills, Helen wanted to stay close to home because Lizzie was not well. Being close allowed Helen to travel to school each day and be home at night and remain as close as she could to Lizzie. Helen had always admired Lizzie!s independence as well as her business experiences. And who could match her experiences as a child riding the prairies with Anna during the Sioux wars. But it was more than that. Lizzie was the ultimate mother, caring, nurturing, and loving but insisting that her children be strong, independent and assertive. Helen could not have a better grandmother as a mentor. Her spiritual connection to the Catholic faith was a gift she had passed on to Ma and Helen and Bob. It would have been so even if Martin had not come to the marriage with Ma as a strong Catholic himself.

Despite excellent medical care and the love of family, Lizzie passed away during Helen!s first semester at Duchene. Ma considered having Lizzie interred near Omaha to be near her, but she decided that Lizzie!s remains would be carried to South Dakota and be interred along side Sam. And so it came to pass, Charles, then Anna, then Sam and finally Lizzie were gone. Ma!s direct side of the family was no longer with her.

They had left their mark in life. Now they were united in death. Martin understood what Lizzie had meant to the family and was grateful to her for all her support and love when he and Ma were first married. He had taken a great deal of time off work to help with Lizzie!s final arrangements. The trip back to Bonesteel allowed him to say his final goodbye to a strong figure in his life as well. The family returned again to Bonesteel that Christmas to again pay respects to Lizzie and to spend some time visiting his parents who were also aging. It was a good time to reminisce about the days of Martin and Ma!s youth, their engagement, marriage and the births of Helen and Bob. Martin and Ma took Helen and Bob to see Doc Schreiber for a checkup and a visit. Following a clean bill of health, Doc showed them his office. Bob was very interested in how it operated and expressed an interest in how one could become a doctor. Doc mentioned that there was a very good medical program at Creighton College in Omaha and Bob kept that information in the back of his mind for future reference. Refreshed and looking ahead with better clarity than weeks before at the funeral service, they returned to Omaha for the next chapter of life.

Martin decided to take another trip after they got back to Omaha. He had remembered his train trip out west and the Rocky Mountains near Denver. He asked Ma whether they would like to go for a few days to Colorado that Spring. Bob was very excited and had spent extra time in the school library researching the Denver area. They went by car and spent nearly a week hiking, fishing and sightseeing. It would be a memorable trip that all would recall the rest of their lives.

When they arrived back in Omaha, Ma gave Helen a letter that had been written several days before Lizzie's death. The handwriting was not very strong but the words were.

Dear Helen,

I am near the end now and felt that you were ready for me to share my last words about your great grandmother and me and what Anna felt was your future. From the day you were born, and even before, she had a vision, a dream maybe, but not just a passing idea, that you would be a warrior like her. As you know from the family tales that she and I took a great journey to the battle of Greasy Grass and joined Sitting Bull, Anna's distant relative to fight for the existence of the Sioux Nation. I saw first-hand the fierceness of Anna's resolve, her piercing gaze. She was not afraid to look someone right in the eyes, sometimes until they looked away. She passed that determination and look on to me and I to your mother. You have that in your blood. I have seen it in your eyes. I know whatever you do, this will serve you well. This will be a part of you that some men will find difficult to embrace. Many seek a mate that they can dominate and rule. But when you find that man who embraces you as you are, keep him close and never let him go.

Anna said to me before she passed away that someday you would take a journey like we did. You would go to lands far away and see great battles and join the fight as warriors do. I did not think much of what she was saying at the time because you were so young when she died. But as I think about the days when I was so young walking along side Anna across the plains, I find myself thinking that you too will find your mission and do what has to be done.

I asked your mother to hold a package for you. Inside you will find the moccasins that Anna made for your birth and the leather pouch that you used to carry the moccasins when you were young. I brought them with us when we moved to Omaha. I had the pouch embroidered by the granddaughter of Martin Redbear with the same beads that decorated your great grandmother's burial dress.

Your mother has raised you well and she has done it with the same love that my mother gave to me and I to my daughter. I know you will share with your children that same love, a mother's love.

My deepest love,

Lizzie

After reading the letter, Ma gave Helen the package that Lizzie had prepared. There, in it was the pouch, beautifully embroidered, and the moccasins. Helen touched them and vowed not to be separated from them. She would keep them with her until she could pass them on to her daughter.

CHAPTER 17

GRADUATION, BAD GUYS AND A GUN
DARK CLOUDS ON THE HORIZON

You might wonder if Martin carried a gun as a Treasury Agent. The answer is that he did. He was well versed in a variety of weapons dating back to his Army days. As an agent, he carried a 38 caliber pistol when he expected trouble. But one thing he had learned from his Army days was a healthy respect for weapons and how accidents can happen. So by choice he always left his pistol locked in the office gun room when he left for home. With Prohibition ending in 1933, the duties of the Treasury Department had changed. Organized Crime was an evolving business and seeing competition for alcohol sales from legitimate businesses increase, it turned to extortion and racketeering, crimes with which it excelled. In early 1939, Martin was asked to join a task force that was sent to Kansas City to tackle the Kansas City Crime Family led by Charles Carollo. The strategy of the task force was to follow the Al Capone model and try to convict Carollo of income tax evasion.

This would be a difficult assignment and a dangerous one. The crime family was given wide berth by the Pendergast Machine, which years later was a political supporter of Harry Truman. The Pendergast Machine during Prohibition had given the predecessors of the Carollo family a free pass from arrests for violation of the Volstead Act. Now that the laws were changed and prosecution for Prohibition violations were not possible, perhaps the crime family!s own records would support a case of federal income tax evasion. Martin and his colleagues knew the Carollo family would not go down easy. They were constantly in fear of assassination when walking the streets of Kansas City. Martin and the team carried their weapons wherever they went. Training at the firing range was a weekly part of the routine. Fortunately, no agents were seriously hurt in the few attempts to disrupt the investigation. Finally, after 6 months of investigation, indictments were brought against the leaders of the Carollo family and Martin could return to Omaha, proud that he had helped bring down a key Midwest crime leader. Once again his pistol was locked in the office gun room.

One thing that Ma had brought with her to Omaha from South Dakota was her skill in caning and preserving fruits. Scattered around the back yard at Erskine Street were flowers and berries as well as plum and peach trees. All were now bearing a good yield. Ma had ordered a supply of mason jars from the Sears Catalog and taught herself how to preserve and store excess fruits from that garden. Soon, with experimenting, she learned to make jelly and jams. Those going through the depression developed strong survival skills and this one was Ma!s. The garden that she worked in Omaha had an abundance of fruit trees and berry plants and were a source of seemingly endless mason jars of preserves and jams.

With Lizzie's death, Helen did not feel compelled to live at home while attending classes at Duchene. She wanted to live on campus and moved into to a rooming house. Whenever she brought a few jars of plum or berry jelly to campus, she was the "toast" of the house. There she roomed with Marjorie Holt and became fast friends with Coreen Ryan and Margaret Wolf. These friendships would last a lifetime. Helen!s studies continued in English, History and French but her education was so well rounded that it prepared her to teach any subject if that is what she wanted to do. As she approached the senior year of college, the world was beginning to change and she learned from everything she read that the European countries that had destroyed each other for nearly 5 years just twenty years before held long seated grudges. Treaty terms that had stripped Germany and had imposed severe reparations fueled the rise of a new government that fed off of nationalism and racism. Some of these themes dated back centuries in Europe. At the same time Japan was expanding its empire fueled by a strong nationalism and belief in the superiority of their culture and race. China and Manchuria had been invaded by Japanese troops and alliances had been made with Germany. Though America was doing its best to struggle out of the depression with various programs, jobs for new graduates were not as plentiful as the period before the depression. Further, opportunities for women graduating from college were even harder to find.

One of the few occupations that women could seek was that of a teacher and Helen was well qualified to teach. She applied for a position and was hired by Elkhorn High School. It was ideal. She could live with Martin and Ma and drive to the school. She had spent the last semester of her Senior year student teaching at Elkhorn. She had been a popular student teacher and she had enjoyed the experience. When she graduated from Duchene, she arranged a small graduation party for her girl friends and classmates. While she had dated off and on through College, none of the men seemed to suit her. Some had become depressed with the future prospects although they were better in 1941 than they had been four years earlier when they had started into College. Helen and her girl friends talked about some day meeting the right guy and being carried off like in the Hollywood movies. But the consensus was that mister right was not going to stroll up the front walk and knock on the door, at least not now. Would their lives be as exciting as it seemed to be for women in the movies? Sure they had the right to vote but careers for single women were rare. At least teaching could provide a living. She and her fellow graduates felt that they could do more in life than just teach.

Helen took an interest in Elkhorn and her students, teaching two subjects, English and History and filling in wherever else she was needed. While not very tall, she was a commanding figure in front of her students. The student teaching had made the prospect of standing in front of a class easier to do. The more she did it, the more confident she became. As Christmas was approaching, she had planned to get something special for her parents. She thought of all the wonders of her Christmases past and how much her parents had made them special. But this Christmas would not be anything like she had imagined.

The war that had seemed so far off in Europe and in China erupted on December 7, 1941. As news of the attack on Pearl Harbor, Hawaii and other military installations in the Pacific, Helen and her three friends gathered in her room listening to the radio broadcast. FDR was talking to the American people to prepare for war. We were at war with Japan. Germany had joined with Japan and declared war on America. Now they were at war in the Pacific and involved in war in Europe. They talked amongst themselves. What was happening, why was this attack made on us and what can we do, Helen and her friends asked each other. We cannot join the Army and fight they agreed. "We have to find a way to make a difference," Helen told the girls. If any of us find a way, they agreed they would all do their part. They had no idea that Christmas what they could really do.

When she returned to teach, she met several of the graduating Seniors, two of whom were brothers of her friends Coreen and Margaret, Bill Ryan and Jim Wolf. At lunch one day, Bill and Jim asked if they could sit with Helen and talk about her father!s service in the Great War. She told them about the experiences of her father, how he had served in the AEF and how he was wounded and was awarded a Purple Heart. He never felt like a fool or a loser for having gone off to war. He knew he could be killed or wounded but it was his country and was proud to serve, she told them. They thanked Helen. She asked them, "Why are you so interested?" They said that they were going to enlist the next day and start to train as soon as possible, even if they had to leave school early. That shook her, knowing that she had not done her best to dissuade them to join up. That weighed heavily on her throughout her teaching career.

Once her two year contract with Elkhorn was finished, she advised the school that she would not return. She told them she had to do something to help end the war. She had seen too many of the young men she had been teaching go off to war and she was not doing her part. She would find something. She had to get into this fight. While many of her students were joining the Marines because they were assured to fight the Japanese who started this thing, Helen felt her language skills might be better used if the US ever got to France. That evening she went home to Martin and Ma and told them some way somehow she would go to war. Martin sat her down and said he understood. He mentioned that Bob was having a hard time at Benson from some of the boys tormenting him because of his German ancestry. It did not seem to make a difference that his father had fought for America against the Germans. Helen was infuriated. She still felt it was her duty to look after Bob. As she paced the room ranting about the nerve of these boys harassing Bob, Ma suggested that Helen think about the Red Cross. She reminded her that she had joined the Red Cross when Martin went to war. Helen said she would investigate.

CHAPTER 18

A GREAT ADVENTURE BEGINS

Helen had done her homework. She had learned the Red Cross was forming a special 5,000 women unit that would be sent in the Summer of 1944 to support the invasion of Europe. Some volunteers were already in England supporting the troops, managing hotels that the US had taken over to house soldiers on leave and running canteens where soldiers could gather, get news from home, listen to music and dance. The entire Red Cross operation would be funded by donations from the American people. By the end of the war over 780 Million Dollars had been raised for Red Cross!s services during the war.

This particular service would be staffed by women who would undergo a high level of screening. Not everyone would be selected. They would be recruited and trained, then shipped to England, and eventually be in the rear echelon of the American Army invading Europe. They were looking for recruits with medical training. But as the mission was to support the morale of the troops through mobile units traveling in the rear, those with skills in driving and logistics were needed. Fortunately, Helen was driving cars and trucks since she was in South Dakota.. Even though she could barely see over the steering wheel of a truck, she was confident she could do what it took to drive the kind of vehicles that the Red Cross would use.

She had gone to the library and got a back issue of the Omaha Herald that contained the writeup on the Red Cross Service plan and brought it home. She sat down in the living room on the piano bench and took Ma!s hands in hers and smiled at Martin. "I am going to Europe and join the fight. I am going to see if my friends will come with me but I am going. I can!t stand the idea of people thinking that the Schonebaum's are not making this fight theirs. I have to do this or I will not be able to stand myself. And I don!t want to hear that I should just settle down and marry someone from Omaha. Anyway, all the good ones are going to war.

I have a better chance on finding the right person if I go away." Martin and Ma agreed with all her reasons and said "It is up to you." Ma asked her to get up off the piano bench. She reached beneath the cover and pulled out a cloth wrapped object and handed it to Helen. In it was a small feather that Ma had received from Anna!s cousins to celebrate the birth of their warrior child the day she was born. "Carry it with you to Europe and join the fight," she told her daughter. Helen found her pouch containing the moccasins and placed the feather in it and would carry them with her throughout the journey.

She contacted Coreen, Margaret and Marjorie and asked them to come to her parent!s house. Helen said she had made up her mind and she was joining the Red Cross and was going to New York. The Red Cross was looking for volunteers to support the troops following the invasion of Europe that Summer. She showed them the article in the Omaha Herald.

Margaret read the article first and said: "Look, no cosmetics, earrings and no bright nail polish!" "Think of all the money we will save!" Helen said. "Hope so because there will be no real money to be earned out of this "volunteer business." Coreen then read the article and looked up and said: "Helen, I don!t even have a driver!s license and I don!t know how to drive a car! They want us to drive jeeps and trucks!" Marjorie said she would go if Helen went but she worried about the age requirement. Helen said, "We can handle the age requirement with the right licenses." Margaret said that she wanted to volunteer for the medical unit as she had worked the last few months at the Omaha medical center as a volunteer. Helen told Coreen, "Don!t worry about driving, I will teach you to drive! In a week we can get you ready to pass your driver!s test." "Let!s start right now," she said. Well, Coreen somehow passed her test in Martin!s car even though the grinding of the gears sounded like the car was falling apart. Helen gently put it back in the garage. She bought the train tickets to New York and they left bound for New York. None of the women had ever been further East than Chicago before so this was all a great adventure. After an overnight stop in Chicago and changing trains they boarded the Limited and off they went to New York. When they arrived at night, a day and a half later, they expected to see bright lights and all the action that New York was known for. They had not realized that New York was finally operating under a mandatory blackout. The government had been requesting that all coastal cities and towns turn off the lights at night because the American ocean going freighters became sitting ducks for German submarines because their silhouettes made them targets. After devastating losses of life and vital war supplies all through 1943, the cities like New York began to comply. The women were unimpressed with what they saw. No flashing lights. It was not as active as Chicago, they thought. Helen had the address of the Red Cross recruiting offices in her hand and off they went following her as if she was a native New Yorker.

They realized the office would be closed and found an inexpensive hotel, the Barbizon hotel, that catered to single women and took a large bedroom which they shared. The next morning, before their first cup of ersatz coffee, they arrived at the Red Cross recruiting offices with their driver!s licenses in hand and Margaret holding her nurses aid credentials in hers. Each was intensely interviewed to determine if they would stand up to the rigors of the anticipated service. Did they have the right personality, would they work well under pressure, were they able to . follow orders and did they appear to be of good moral character. Only one in six women met the standards and were accepted. All of Helen!s companions were convincing enough to meet these standards and their licenses all reflected they met the minimum age requirement. They then underwent physicals but when the Doctor looked at Helen, he said, "I don!t know if you meet the height qualifications." Helen reached in her purse and grabbed a pair of socks, folded them over and slipped them into her shoes and passed the physical with flying colors. Yes, she was small in stature but nothing was going to stop her. She was a bundle of energy and was about to be unleashed on the enemy. They were bused to Pennsylvania Station and boarded a train for Washington DC where a training facility had been established at the campus of American University. They were issued uniforms and began the physical training.

Margaret was assigned to a medical training unit; the other three women were assigned to a six person tent with Army cots and blankets. Outdoor showers and a mess hall constituted the home base for the women. There was one large tent that could handle chairs and benches for 30 women. There they would learn their roles, their mission and work on their skills. They were shown a mock-up of the truck that was used to transport coffee, donuts and refreshments to the troops near the front.

They called them Clubmobiles. These trucks were equipped with machines that could make hundreds of donuts an hour. Helen would recall years later that she made so many donuts that the sight of one turned her stomach. These trucks would allow them to be mobile and move from camp to camp away from the direct fighting. They were taught that in war the lines of battle were fluid and there were no safe areas really. What was an area behind the front could be in the middle of a battle or an artillery bombardment in the next minute. They were told, "Always be prepared to move and quickly!" They were instructed that, next to the coffee, donuts and refreshments, the troops always needed extra socks, gloves and caps for warmth. "Never mind that it is Spring and early Summer now. This war will last into the Winter and you will be there!" They learned to drive the trucks and jeeps that the

Red Cross would be assigned. Helen drove like a pro but the instructors always had to check and see if anyone was behind the wheel. Helen!s group was certified, received their Red Cross Pins and were assigned a departure date from Brooklyn. That night she composed a short letter to her parents.

Dear Martin and Ma,

As you know from my telegram last month, all us girls arrived and made it into the Red Cross. We have been through intensive training, received, proudly, our Red Cross pins and will be shipping out for our destination in the next few days. Just as our military is secretive about the destinations of troop movements, I cannot tell you where our first stop will be. But as our Army is preparing to invade Europe soon, I expect we will be following the guys soon. I don!t want you to be worried for me. I will be fine. We met another woman from upper New York and she will be traveling with the unit Coreen, Marjorie and I are with. She is Ester Castleman. Margaret will be with the medical unit that we will be attached to. I am looking forward to putting my French studies to use and to see all the things you did not see in France when you were there. Say a prayer for us.

We will for you.

Love,

Helen

CHAPTER 19

ENGLAND

The Red Cross volunteers had been told that they would first land in England and then be shipped to France, following the Army. The voyage would be on the Queen Mary, which had been before the war, an elegant, luxury vessel. But it had been converted to troop transport and had been repainted and stripped of all ornamentation unnecessary to transport people quickly and without frills. Upon first gaze, Helen concluded that it looked nothing like an elegant luxury passenger vessel. She knew that the U-Boats still prowled the Atlantic and was shocked to see that the Mary was completely unarmed. One of the crew reassured her that the Mary was one of the fastest vessels afloat and that no U-Boat could match its speed. "Nevertheless, Miss, here is your life jacket which should be worn at all times you are outside of your cabin". Not completely reassuring, she thought! She had not considered this aspect of the adventure and she hoped that they would at least get into the war theater rather than go down with the ship before they even began. Typically, a fast passenger liner would take 4 days to sail from New York to Bristol England. But because the ship traveled in a convoy with freighters and troop ships, accompanied by escort vessels, usually destroyers, the voyage lasted 6 full days. The convoy could expect to receive air protection for the first third and last third of the voyage but during the middle leg of the voyage, the ships were beyond the range of air cover. That was when the nail biting would begin. Although the weather was expected to be better in a Summer crossing, the women were still seasick. Boating in freshwater ponds did not prepare them for a sea voyage. Helen remembered that Martin said some soldiers had kissed the sand when they arrived in France because they were so grateful to get off their transport. Helen understood why.

They arrived in Bristol the evening of the sixth day of the voyage and were met by a caravan of British lorries that took them to the Red Cross Headquarters near Bath. They had a week before the brigade would be formally organized and the now five women formed a plan to see as much of the area that they could. They dressed in the civilian clothes they brought to England with them and sampled the local gardens, the towns around Bath, the local pubs and tasted differ types of English food. They took one long day to visit London which they reached by train. They saw a few sights including Buckingham palace, Westminster and the Parliament building. They found an air raid shelter and waited out an air raid. Exhausted they returned to the training facility at Bath, making the early morning formation dressed in their proper uniforms.

They formed into their assigned ranks and were inspected. Helen stood at the far right of her line, the shortest of the brigade and very much in charge of her line which in the Red Cross was the equivalent of a platoon. The newly assigned commander of the brigade thought about calling her a midget but after seeing her energy and leadership dubbed her "Midge" and the nickname just stuck. The next morning four girls from Omaha and another from Upper New York joined the brigade and boarded lorries and set out for France.

CHAPTER 20

THE CAPTAIN
PRIVATE TO CAPTAIN

Bert Waller was from Tiawah, Oklahoma, a small town east of Tulsa. At the age of 16 and not quite 17, he had enlisted in the Army joining the artillery stationed at Ft Sill, OK. He started out as an enlisted soldier and not having finished high school, the prospects of higher advancement in America!s peacetime Army were nonexistent. But he felt he had little choice because of the circumstances with his family, he had to find a job that might be long term career. His father, a law enforcement officer in Oklahoma, had just been slain in a shootout with a criminal suspect, leaving his mother with limited resources and too many mouths to feed. The Army offered a steady income and a future. He could send money home to his mother Nell. His older brothers had done the same and he would pitch in and help the family. But he was not to remain a private forever. The skills necessary for an artilleryman were so much more than loading a field piece, pulling a trigger and unloading the piece. It involved map reading, mathematical skills, estimating distance, range and trajectory and reacting quickly to adjustment to information and recalculating for the same or another target. Despite his limited high school education, he was adept at all of this. The brass in charge of the Ft. Sill artillery division were well aware of what was happening in Europe and the Pacific. They stepped up training, made sure they had equipment that was in proper condition and made sure their ranks were filled with trained personnel. By 1940 this young lad had obtained his high school equivalency degree and advanced to the rank of sergeant. His platoon were aware that his lineage had strong traces of Cherokee blood and referred to him as Chief behind his back rather than Sgt. Elbert "Bert" Waller. He knew of his moniker and it did not bother him. He took it as a sign of respect. Derogatory names were just part of the military at the time. He supposed there were worse nicknames that he could be called. By the Summer of 1941, Bert had secured enough recommendations and applied for Officer Candidate School. Successful graduates earned the rank of a Second Lieutenant but were subject of being placed in a branch other than he was serving at the time of application. Fortunately, the artillery was the best fit and by the time Pearl Harbor was attacked, he graduated and received his commission in the artillery.

Although war against Germany was formally declared in December 1941, it would take months to recruit and draft, equip and train hundreds of thousands of soldiers needed to conduct a campaign. Bert!s division, the Ninth Artillery was an existing unit that had trained together but few had any combat experience, other than some of the executive officers. Moreover, the entire Army needed a strategy, a plan and logistics necessary to move from the desire to fight to conducting actual operations in Europe or anywhere else. Further, England and the few remaining allies had definite ideas about where and when operations would be conducted. It was not until November 1942 that Bert and the rest of the Ninth Artillery Division hit the beaches in North Africa as part of Operation Torch. By the Summer of 1944, his artillery unit had participated in victories in North Africa and Sicily and had supported the invasion of Italy. Now the Ninth was in England, recuperating, resting, being resupplied, receiving replacements, training and formed to participate in the D-Day operations. By now the young Second Lieutenant had been promoted to First Lieutenant. His combat duties ranged from commanding forward observation units to fire and control duties. The Ninth Artillery hit the beaches of Normandy at D-Day plus 2 and were in the fight all the way through VE Day. By the end of the war in Europe, millions had joined and fought. Many families sacrificed sons in both the European campaign and in the Pacific and many families saw multiple sons and daughters serve their country. In Bert!s case, all five of his brothers and his sister served in uniform. By VE Day, Bert was a Captain.

CHAPTER 21

FRANCE

Although the Red Cross was an all-volunteer unit it was always understood that they were under the command of the US Army. It was important that all logistics of the support for the troops be coordinated to make the support operations most efficient. The Army would identify areas where the Clubmobile trucks would go, the roads to be taken, the areas to avoid and how long they could stay. The Clubmobile trucks were driven by women and the coffee, donut and refreshments were handed out efficiently and orderly. An updated collections of magazines and newspapers would be carried so that current news would be available to the troops. Chairs and tables as well as shelters would be set up to make the experience different from the front. Portable record players were carried in the trucks and set up to play current tunes to remind the soldiers of home. Many of the soldiers would sit and read the letters that came from home that had finally caught up to them at the camps in the rear. Some soldiers who had difficulty reading would ask the Red Cross personnel to read to them which was a great comfort to the servicemen. Others would seek help in writing back home and the women were only too happy to help. It is estimated that these tireless women throughout all theaters of war helped servicemen with over 42,000,000 messages to and from folks back home.

The one thing that the women had some reservations about were cigarettes. The Army had kept the soldiers well supplied with free cigarettes in their rations and the Clubmobiles were well stocked. After a while even the women were smoking. No one thought about how bad these things were for you then.

In order not to overwhelm the women, the trucks would be staffed with a minimum of eight and travel in convoys of 3 or 4 vehicles. Women drove the trucks, with a rotating crew of three drivers. They had to know how to service the vehicles in case of a breakdown, although the central dispatching location near Rouen did have a service crew of mechanics. Midge was in charge of her crew and Coreen was one of the rotating team of drivers. Roads were not great but Midge had the knowledge to rock her truck out of ditches, jumpstart a vehicle when the battery was low and change a tire. Knowing how to do a repair was one thing, marshaling all eight women to push a vehicle out of a ditch or place a wheel in place when changing a flat is another. But frequently an Army vehicle would come along and pitch in to get them back on the road. This was no small feat as these tires were almost as high as Midges chest.

Marjorie was the expert operating the donut machine and the coffee pots. In the first few weeks of operation in Northern France, Midge team reported that they simply could not make enough donuts to supply the troops. They suggested that the dispatching location near Rouen set up a bakery so that an adequate supply of donuts and baked goods would be available. This proved to be a practical solution.

Just because the Army was giving orders directing the Clubmobiles to follow specified roads, there was no assurance that all would be safe and free from the action of battle. Though the maps showed territory in the hands of the Allies, no one could rule out isolated pockets of enemy soldiers. While the air was dominated by American and British fighters, occasional German fighters would appear unexpectedly overhead. The vehicles were marked with a red cross, but it seemed this marked them as targets rather than noncombatants. There had been casualties among the women driving out of Rouen and Midge remembered the words of her trainers back in Washington, "always be prepared". They were far enough back from the front to avoid a stray artillery shell but an aircraft was not out of the question. Of bigger concern were unexploded ordinance and land mines. These simply could not be seen from behind the wheel of a truck or a jeep.

Setting out that August morning, something was bothering Midge. She went through her checklist she used to plan each trip, checked her map and called to the back of the truck to make sure all was right. "Stop worrying" she thought. She had heard just that morning that Paris had surrendered to the Allies. Someday soon she would get to see the city that her father had not two decades before. Then she saw, well up ahead of their convoy, six German soldiers. Midge stopped the convoy and ordered everyone out of the trucks and into a nearby ditch. The trucks drew fire and the women stayed under cover. Suddenly, Midge heard a jeep coming from the opposite direction they were heading. The driver and officer riding beside him saw what was happening stopped and pulled their sidearms and fired off a few shots at the Germans, who at that point stopped firing and raised their hands, dropped their weapons and shouted "nein scheuss"! The Americans asked if there were any donuts in the trucks. Midge asked how many they wanted? She noted a few might have a few more holes in them and they could have as many as they wanted. The officer gave a few to the captured Germans and put a few in the jeep. He thanked Midge and suggested they might want to return to Rouen. Midge, noted his rank as Captain, and she and her crew thanked the Americans, turned the trucks around and drove back to Rouen. Donuts would not be delivered to troops this day.

Upon their return to Rouen, Midge and her crew checked with the Commander and confirmed that Paris had surrendered on August 25 and that the Germans that had not surrendered were fleeing towards the Belgian and German borders driving whatever they could and running where vehicles were not to be found. Midge reported her incident to her Commander and the capture of some stragglers by a brave American Captain and his driver. Another assignment was given to Midge. This time the trip was in the opposite direction and the Clubmobile was well received by the American troops. While casualties were infrequent, 52 of the women serving with the Red Cross were wounded in the European theater, some seriously. Midge and her crew were fortunate that no one was hurt in her encounter and that the Clubmobiles were not seriously damaged in the fight. These women were not armed and their safety depended on the protection of the American troops in the vicinity of the camps and along the routes of travel. The fact that there was good coordination between the Red Cross units and the Army kept the casualties low. That night Midge had a strange dream revisiting the surprise on the road that morning. She dreamt about the nameless Captain. As the dream began to get erotic, she awoke with a start. She might have to talk about that with a priest if she ever had time to get to church.

Every evening after duty the Commander would gather the women together and ask the second in command to hand out any mail that the

Brigade had received. Mail from the States usually took four or five weeks to arrive depending on the point of dispatch. Much traveled by ship to England and then was sorted and transported, in the Red Cross's case to the applicable unit location. As Midge relaxed in the back row, she heard her name called out. She paused and slowly walked up to the front and took her envelop. It was somewhat embarrassing. Some girls got letters every week from boys back home or boys they had met in France. She was puzzled as she had none of these. This letter was from Ma.

Darling Helen,

Martin and I are so relieved to learn of your safe arrival in England and have followed the planned invasion of France.

We know that you are doing the right thing supporting our guys over there. It is an important thing you are doing but we are both praying nothing happens to you and that you will be safe from harm. Once you left, Martin and I talked about all his experiences in France in more detail than we ever have before. The terrors of war, he told me, had kept many of his terrible memories locked away. It has always been a dark area for him and I hope nothing like that happens with you. But know we are here for you, always.

Bob will soon finish Medical School and has joined the Army as a medical officer. It will be a while before they activate him or send him anywhere but he wanted you to know that he is praying for you. He wanted to remind you about the war games you both played in the plowed fields of Bonesteel. He said to "keep your head down".

It is difficult for us with you being so far away but we raised you to be independent and strong. We are confident that you will come back to us soon.

All our love,

Ma

After over two months of continuous service without a day off, Midge and her crew were ordered relieved for two weeks. By the end of September, Paris was clear and was THE destination for not only the Red Cross personnel but many of the troops who also had some badly needed R&R. Midge, Coreen, Ester and Marjorie were off to Paris.

CHAPTER 22

PARIS

Midge drove a jeep that had been assigned to the Red Cross with Marjorie, Ester and Coreen on board. They checked into the La Masson hotel that had been reserved for senior officers and members of the Red Cross. A canteen had been set up in the sun room of the hotel. Some of the staff servicing the canteen had trained with Midge and her crew in Washington, DC and they were made welcome. "*Boogie Woogie Bugle Boy*" was playing in the background and they all sat down with their sisters while their rooms were being readied. Unlike their stay in New York and all their accommodations since arriving in France, they each got their own room with their own bathroom. Paradise! Midge had parked the jeep in a military lot so that it would be secure. While parking the jeep, she thought she saw the sergeant that had ridden to their rescue just a few weeks ago but she just missed him. No sign of the Captain.

After a long lunch they set out for a walking tour of Paris. After more than three years of occupation by the Germans, Paris was undergoing a vibrant awakening. Cars that had been stored away in barns and garages around the city were gradually resurfacing. Parisians were wearing some of their finer clothes. Midge noted that there were a few women who were wearing head scarves that Coreen said hid very short hair. Ester said that they had been accused of sleeping with the enemy and had their heads shaved in retribution for their fraternization. The women stared at them and then looked away. They arrived at the edge of the Seine and looked across the bridge at the island that held the Cathedral of Notre Dame. They bounded across the bridge arm in arm, found a head cover for each of them and reverently entered the Cathedral. They toured the church noting all the hand carved wood and the stained glass windows. Midge spotted an open confessional, thought a moment and then got in line. A French woman standing in front of her, observing she was American, pointed out a sign indicating confessions were heard only in French. Midge thanked her with her best French, "merci beau coup," and waited her turn. Aside from missing Sunday Mass since her crew arrived in France, she had frequent dreams about her Captain that had rescued her several days ago and she could not shake it. Also she had received recently letters from home that revealed some of her former high school students had returned to Omaha with severe wounds. One, Billy Ryan, Coreen!s younger brother had died. Coreen!s grief had lasted for days but Coreen was dealing with it better now. A confession and a conversation with a priest might put Midge in a better frame of mind. The idea that she had somehow not discouraged Billy from signing up to fight haunted her.

Notre-Dame de Paris, which means Our Lady of Paris, was the symbol of Paris and the French people. On the hour, the famous bells, that in the imagination of Victor Hugo were rung by the deaf hunchback Quasimodo, called out the time of day. The interior of the Cathedral was unlike any church any of the women had seen in America. The wood was carved into beautiful images of biblical scenes and surrounded the altars. Candles were lit all around the cathedral illuminating spaces that would otherwise be in darkness. Curiously, many of the important pieces of art were missing as they referred to their tour guides written in the prewar era. They learned that many were removed and hidden from the invading German army five years before. What was there was beautiful. They al agreed it was worth visiting. On leaving, they looked back at the

Cathedral one last time. Then they shouted, "On to the Louvre!" First they stopped in a bistro and each ordered a glass of wine. These women were all from small towns or cities and wine was something that they were not used to. It was a special treat for them, but having spent the last few months drinking coffee and water, the wine took some getting used to. Aside from getting used to a foreign drink, they took in all the sights along the Seine. The river gently floated by and there were a few boaters enjoying the day.

The Louvre museum was reopened on a limited basis. Many of the world renown works of art that were not hidden before the fall of France had been stolen by the Germans during the occupation and more as the Germans fled the city in August. But these American women were thrilled to be there and to see whatever was still in the rooms that were open for viewing. The highlight of the visit was viewing the Mona Lisa. They did not know that what they saw was not the original painting which the curators had evacuated along with over 3,000 other world renown paintings and art works in August and September 1939. It was a copy. The actual painting was not returned until June 1945. They strolled up the Champ Elysees, stopping at a few open cafes and looking up the street towards the Arch d Triumph. They remembered the Newsreel movies at the theater back home that showed the French lined up on the streets crying as the German troops marched in triumph as they entered Paris in 1939. Maybe this war will end someday, they thought. They had done the right thing being a part of all of this. They were in the fight, not with guns or bombs, but supporting the guys morale. Maybe it would be enough. They returned to the hotel for a nap and a dinner on the town.

That afternoon, Midge wrote her first real letter home to her parents since she got to France. The Telegram from Piccadilly Square in London did not count. She had thought about a postcard from London but the cost was too much for just a card. While serving in the Red Cross was a volunteer position, the Red Cross gave each person a stipend that helped offset their expenses and allowed them some spending money while on leave. None of the women did their jobs for money. It was their duty.

Dear Martin and Ma,

I miss you both and am well and here in Paris! I am so fortunate to have chosen to be part of the Red Cross Service Brigade. I feel that I am really serving our great country and am doing my part to boost the morale of our troops. If you could see the look of gratitude in their eyes when they come to our canteens and connect with home you would know why I am so happy I decided to do this. Margaret has really been doing a great job supporting the medical units. Coreen, Marjorie and our friend from New York, Ester have been traveling with me around France bringing coffee, donuts and refreshments to the troops. We are pretty safe doing this with only one close call so far. I had my feather with me. I am so grateful that Martin taught me to drive. I usually do the driving for my crew and am very confident with my skills.

I have been able speak French with the locals and they actually understand me. We can converse and I have learned so much about food and customs and the history of the region. I even spoke at length in French with a priest at the Cathedral of Notre Dame. All of us are now in Paris and Martin, I want you to remember how much we talked about your experiences in France during the Great War and how much I wanted someday to see Paris. And now I am here with my best friends. It is quite a place even though the evidence that the Germans had occupied this place for four years is still clear. I am going to get an inexpensive camera, if I can, and take pictures of this adventure. The Eiffel Tower is where we are going tomorrow.

One place I want to visit before I leave France is the Abbey at St. Michel. You remember Martin, it was in the box of pictures that you bought and gave me on my 16th Birthday. I remember the stereograph device you bought so we could see the pictures in more than one dimension. Will get a souvenir from there if I can.

Your loving daughter,
Helen

The crew spent the remainder of their leave in Paris, eating, walking and seeing the sights, dancing at the canteen and just taking in the atmosphere of Paris. As they were sitting in the restaurant the morning they had to leave Paris, Coreen came dashing in excitedly and told them that there was a hair salon that had just reopened next door to the hotel and that they were specializing in a new style, the "Paris Look". "Anyway, she said, "we all look like sheepdogs and need a cut before we go back. I reserved time for all of us this morning so we are going." Midge eyes lit up and they all marched out of the hotel following Coreen to the salon. It was a great way to end the short stay in Paris. Fortunately, none of them had the beautician apply any makeup on as it was against regulations for Midge and her crew to apply excessive makeup while on duty. Their hair did become the talk of the Brigade.

They had not realized how fatigued they were when they first arrived and sleeping was high on their agenda during their stay. When they arrived back in Rouen refreshed and ready to resume their duties, their commander told them that their unit had been transferred to a new command center just north of Paris. They could not believe their ears. They could spent as much time as they could in and around Paris. In November they moved their command center to Reims which was Northeast of Paris and closer to the Belgium border and to the front. Scuttlebutt had the Allies winning the war by the end of 1944 and the women were looking forward to following the troops into Germany. They had purchased a few German-French-English translation books. But as they poured over the newspapers and in particular the Stars and Stripes, the optimism was there but not with the certainty that the scuttlebutt was repeating. Midge began to see that supplies were becoming short, particularly in the motor pools that the women relied upon to maintain their vehicles. Maybe that was the reason for the rumors. It made sense not to oversupply the war effort if the end was really close. But if supplies were cut back too far, we might not make it to the end whenever that was, she thought.

The routine continued for the women but now there were many new faces that were being added to the command. Some of the crews were shuffled around so that the experience of the first crews could be spread around. Much of their time before mid-December was spent training the new arrivals. In her training sessions Midge continued to stress being prepared for surprises but she was afraid that her warnings were falling on deaf ears. The Allies were going to win this. That is what everyone thought. Then all hell broke loose.

CHAPTER 23

IT'S NOT OVER YET

The Red Cross issued all the women in November another uniform that someone high up in the Red Cross thought was more suitable for the coming winter: wool skirts and warm jackets! There were a few with woolen sweaters but uniforms that included long wool slacks were few and far between. Officials of the Red Cross felt that the morale of the soldiers was more important than the creature comfort of the women trying their best to support the men. Maybe they were thinking we were working indoors, Midge and her crew thought! Even if that were the case, few of the temporary buildings housing the vehicles and offices were heated at all. But we are all outdoors, thought Midge and she was having none of wearing skimpy clothes in the dead of winter. She stalked into the Army quartermaster!s office in Reims and demanded as many pairs of Army issued woolen trousers as they had in small sizes. These the quartermaster had an excess supply of and, after a good stare from Midge and the word "NOW" from Midge, he parted with two dozen pairs. Midge!s crew spent the next few days trimming and sewing the trousers into suitable leg coverings for her crew and two others. It would get them through until correct leggings arrived. Some of these trousers were worn right through Spring!

By the middle of December, the weather had turned very cold and the area north of Reims was seeing a good snowfall. Midge and her crew along with two other two other Clubmobiles headed to the rear echelon locations at the rear of the First and Ninth Armies. It was 9 days before Christmas and Midge had collected several recordings of Christmas music to play on the portable record player. Due to the cold, they were having a difficult time making the fresh donuts. Nothing stayed warm, not the donuts or the coffee. Because of the wind and snow, Midge elected to serve the soldiers right from the Clubmobile. Suddenly Midge noticed the soldiers were leaving and heading out of the rear back towards the front. "What is going on," she said. Then to the north she could hear thunder or something that sounded like it. But it was snowing, it could not be thunder, Midge reasoned. It must be explosions. Then she saw the familiar face of her Captain who was shouting for them to pack up and get out. The Germans were mounting an attack and advancing. "Move! Move!" he said. Midge made sure her crew was on board and cranked up the engine. "My God, the Germans must be mounting some sort of attack. This war is not over yet!" she said.

Midge sped out of the encampment towards Reims but looked back to see Coreen!s truck was nowhere in sight. She halted the caravan and turned around and went back. Coreen was standing on the bumper of her truck fiddling with the engine. She yelled, "It won!t start!" Midge shouted, "Get in and I will get behind and give you a push. Maybe the battery is just low!" Coreen!s crew got out and huddled near a stone wall.

The explosions seemed to be coming closer. They certainly were louder. Now they could hear the returning artillery fire from the American guns. Maybe this might turn out all right. With a push from Midge!s truck and a roll down the hill in gear, Coreen!s engine fired up. Coreen loaded up her crew and drove down the road toward Reims, following Midge. They had not gone a mile when the road ahead was closed. A stream of jeeps and trucks was pouring North on the road towards the front to reinforce against the German breakthrough. The Clubmobile caravan pulled over and stayed where they were, in no man!s land. Soon they became an island of refuge as wounded soldiers gravitated to the Red Cross markings on their trucks. The women leapt into action, patching wounded soldiers and caring for those whose wounds seemed beyond repair. Midge, Coreen and Marjorie had directed the response. After a few hours doing whatever they could, Midge saw that the road was reopened. She ordered the convoy to dump the donut machines and all excess cargo from the trucks and lift every wounded soldier onto the vehicles. Then they headed for Reims. The wounded were left at the First Aid Station on the way and Midge safely arrived in Reims, her unit intact, but without the valuable donut makers. Shortly after they had flopped on their bunks, they received orders to evacuate to Paris. They helped strike the tents and load vehicles and Midge and the Brigade drove south to Paris. For the next three weeks, Midge and her crew listened to radio reports and poured over the newspaper articles on what was being called the "Battle of the Bulge".

The German intended to surprise the Americans that had slowed their advances from France into the Low Countries. After the ill-fated Market Garden offensive into Holland, the Allied forces took time to regroup and prepare for winter. But winter clothing was lacking and supplies were short. The American supply chain was in reality being managed as if the war was nearly over. The Americans initially were routed by the German attack. Certainly there were old men and boys from Germany in the ranks, but among the German forces were elite troops and superior armored vehicles. They had caught the Americans by surprise. But the Americans desperately held on, eventually halting the German offensive. One key battle was in Bastogne in Luxembourg. The Americans in Bastogne were surrounded and refused to surrender eventually being relieved by elements of Patton!s Third Army. The German offensive, which started on December 16, 1944, initially involved over 400,000 men, over 1,000 tanks and aircraft and 2,600 pieces of artillery. Many of these men had escaped France after the

D-Day invasion and Allied breakout in July 1944 as well as soldiers that had escaped the surrender of Paris. Nearly one fourth of the German forces were killed or wounded. Against this offensive there were over 600,000 Allied soldiers.

Casualties were heavy with nearly 20,000 deaths. The western most advance of the German Army was the village of Foy-Notre-Dame in Belgium. When the skies cleared and the Allied aircraft could take to the air, the end of the offensive was at hand.

As January came to a close the Red Cross Service Brigade was back in full action following the Allied offensives toward Germany. By the end of March 1945, both the Americans and the British had crossed the Rhine River and entered German soil. Back at their base camp Midge and the women kept pace with the day to day advances. The donut machines they had pitched at the beginning of the battle had been replaced. The commander had thought about reprimanding Helen's unit for the loss but Helen stared her down and it was forgotten.

One story that the Stars and Stripes was reporting was the existence of concentration camps. The German government had, since the mid 1930!s, been arresting and detaining political opponents and then Jews and others that the Nazi's deemed undesirables such as homosexuals and gypsies, all in an effort to create a Master Race. Rather than deport these people, the Hitler regime began the systematic annihilation of the Jews from all countries allied with them and all the countries they had occupied such as France. This was well known by all the Allies but the magnitude of the horror was not known until the Allies defeated German forces in Poland and Germany. When she read the report in the Stars and Stripes, she wondered if there was anything the Red Cross Service Brigade could do.

That night she wrote home.

Dear Martin and Ma,

I am taking a break for a few days. We have been following Patton and his army is now in Germany. Imagine a young German American girl entering the country of her grandmother's birth with an army intending to defeat their armies. It is clear from everything I have seen that their army has done horrible things to the people of the countries they have invaded. The people we have freed in France, Belgium and Holland have rejoiced to be free of evil. It embarrasses me that people with the same blood as me could be part of the pure evil that has been visited on these peoples. I fear that I will see more evil than we Americans can ever comprehend as we drive deeper into Germany. From the reports we hear, there are camps where Jews were imprisoned all over Germany and other countries Germany had conquered. Whether we will see them, I do not know. How could this happen? All the Germans I ever knew in Bonesteel or Omaha were gentle people without hate. What caused the people from Grandmom Anna Kapleman's homeland to behave in this way, I will never know.

I have been through a lot in the last few months with my crew. We fled the German forces who had surprised our forces in the Argonne in what they call the Battle of the Bulge. Martin, I remember the war stories you told me with reluctance as I picked your memories of your experiences in the Great War. Our boys in this Battle suffered greatly and we were nearly caught in the whole battle. Fortunately, an officer that I had met before got us out of the area before it was overrun. I hope I see him again but things change and the scope of this campaign is so vast that I doubt it will happen. I know his division is with Patton's army. I will update you if I see him again. When I went through the Argonne after the battle, sections of the woods were so thick, you could not see very far at all. Locals said it was unchanged since before the Great War. Fighting there was unimaginable to me.

Hope you are both well. I think this will end soon but I fear that the Fuhrer will fight to the end. We can only pray. May God bless our troops. Thank God we had FDR to lead us through this war.

Just a word more. Have not met anyone yet worth this journey but I am still certain I am no worse off than I would be if I stayed home in Omaha. Have not really been looking but there are a lot of fine young men sacrificing all they have for this war and our country. Maybe if one really shows an interest, I do not think I could go wrong with the right guy that loves his country as I do.

Love,

Helen

It was just a week or so later, on April 12, 1945, that Franklin Roosevelt, the thirty-second President of the United States died. Word spread quickly through the American forces. Midge heard it over the Armed Forces radio that evening as she was sitting down for dinner. All sat silently listening attentively as they absorbed the news. Harry Truman would have big shoes to fill and she hoped he was up to the task. This war was not over yet. The Russians were on the outskirts of Berlin but Germany was not conquered yet. There were many tears that night but as Midge looked around the table, the faces of the women in her crew showed deep determination. They were part of this fight and would see it through until the end.

CHAPTER 24

OCCUPATION AND BEYOND

Berlin was under siege and Eisenhower elected not to slug it out door to door letting the Soviet Army bring Germany to its knees. It made sense to Americans as the cost of taking Berlin would be high in terms of deaths and wounded. Directives from Washington had been received that required Eisenhower to cede responsibility to capture Berlin to the Russians. The Ninth, after crossing the Rhine in March steadily marched eastward and continued to accept the surrender of German forces along the way. They drove on into Bavaria. Midge!s Red Cross Service Brigade followed at a safe distance behind. Finally, the Army halted after being confronted by the Dachau concentration camp. The Army placed strict control over information, not wanting to release anything about the site until the brass understood what was involved with the camp. When the medical officers arrived and the horrors were evident, the Commander ordered the nearby villages to be forcibly marched to the camp and be confronted by the tragedy. Nearly every one of the villagers feinted ignorance of the existence of the camp, the gas chambers and the crematoriums. They may not have acknowledged responsibility, but they could never deny that it happened. Soldiers were called upon to give assistance to the survivors but many were frightened by the walking dead and fear of disease. A call went back to the Red

Cross Service Brigade and medical units, supported by the service units were brought to the front to assist. Midge and Margaret's crews came when called. They came to the camps and were as shocked as the soldiers had been. The horror was worse than they could have imagined. The survivors were so gaunt that they were barely human. How could any man do this to another. Many of the survivors were children. Again the horror of all this was unimaginable. Helen and Margaret were working together again and the task was gruesome. The initial reaction of the first to respond to the starving survivors was to feed them. Not having eaten much over the past few years and deprived of calories, attempts to feed them large quantities of food was detrimental to those barely holding onto life. Gradual feeding proved to be best, a lesson that the Red Cross would apply for generations wherever they found poverty and starvation throughout the world. What proved to be a cruel irony was that these survivors had lost their homes and their families and were still in the middle of a battle zone. They were safer staying in place inside the same barbed wire fences that had enslaved them for years. The Ninth went from liberators to wardens. That ate on the conscience of the officers and enlisted men as much as the initial sight of the camp. Midge and Margaret were overwhelmed at the task before them. Midge looked up and thought she saw a familiar face among a group of officers. Yes, it was her Captain from France and he was still an artillery officer with the Ninth directing the rescue operations. Despite heroic acts of those aiding in the rescue, many died in the aftermath of surviving. It seemed like a hopeless task, helping the survivors live and then realizing most had no home to return to.

That night the reports came into the service brigade headquarters in Fulda, not only of Hitler!s death by suicide in a bunker in Berlin, but of the unconditional surrender of all German forces. After what Midge and her crew had seen at the camp, it was hard to celebrate with great joy. The war was over in Europe but would continue in the Pacific for another four months. The role of the US Army in Germany changed from a conqueror to an occupier, from a warrior to a peacekeeper and from an armed soldier to law enforcement. Major towns and geographic centers were assigned to officers that had demonstrated organizational skills and leadership qualities. Within a time after the surrender, Captain Waller was assigned by US Military Command to be commandant of the town of Berchtesgaden in Bavaria. Nearby was the Red Cross Service Brigade command center. In a few months many of Midge!s fellow service personnel elected to end their service and return to the US. Many stayed to help with the millions of displaced people throughout Germany and Europe. Those that served in support of a victory in a war that lasted four years returned to the US. Despite their service, unlike the nurses and medical personnel, Midge's fellow service personnel did not receive recognition, medals or special commendations or financial rewards or preferential treatment for jobs or even get to keep their uniforms. They kept their Red Cross pins and handed them down to their daughters. Their stories are not told in books or portrayed in movies, perhaps because they did their jobs without shooting a gun or dropping a bomb or healing a wound. It was an important job and someone had to do it and they had done it.

But some stayed in Europe continuing to support the troops and to effect the expanded duties of the Red Cross. In the initial time after Occupation was underway, many of the soldiers married and either had children or adopted their spouses children. The Red Cross undertook the education and assimilation of over 20,000 war brides by the end of 1949. That involved teaching English, educating the future brides how to buy goods and services, the American currency system, how to write checks and all the practical aspects of American life.

Midge and her Omaha friends agreed to stay a while in Germany and take necessary leaves and see parts of Europe that they might never see again in their lifetimes. Midge took a leave to England where she picked up many simple recipes that she would prepare many, many times. They continued to run the canteen near Berchtesgaden and the Saturday night dances. Then on Christmas Eve of 1946, Captain Waller, commandant of Berchtesgaden entered the Fulda canteen. He was really good looking, stood ramrod straight in his dress uniform, spoke well and had a gentle nature to him. This was not what Midge had remembered when he had shouted for them to move out of harm's way back during the Battle of the Bulge. She walked up to him, taking him by surprise at her directness. She stuck out her hand and thanked him for his assistance two times.

"What?" he asked. As she related both incidents, he suggested that it might have been him but he could not say it was definitely him. Midge introduced her crew and thanked him for coming to the dance. Bert asked Midge if he could have the honor of a dance. She told him, "Of course!" They created a stir when they danced together across the floor. When the next song was played, they stayed together talking and then they danced again. Once Bert danced that first dance with Midge, he would only dance with Midge. Bert walked Midge to the refreshment stand and they began to talk about life before their respective service. He told her that he was from Indian country in Oklahoma and she told him she had come from South Dakota but her folks lived in Omaha. She said that but for this God awful war they might never have met. He said something strange to her then. He said, "I don!t know. I think that someway somehow we were meant to meet". She had not ever had someone so nice become so direct so fast. She liked this man even if it was not he that had rescued her several times in the war. He was the kind of man that her father would like. "Midge," he said, would you like to go to dinner at the Chateau in Berchtesgaden next Friday night?" He told her that the meals were prepared by the Army chef and that there would be several officers and staff present. Midge accepted on the spot, asking, "What time by the way?" He said "I will pick you up at 6, dinner is at 6:30 sharp." The courtship was torrid and fast. They became steady dinner companions and if there was a band playing somewhere they would find a dance floor. After a few great dinners and long walks through the small berg of Berchtesgaden, Bert stopped in the plaza and asked her a question. He asked her, "Could you, I mean, would you consider marrying a soldier?" She said that she wanted to take a little time to answer. Bert did not know what to think. They drove back to her barracks in silence.

The next day Midge went into her commander and asked for a leave for her and Coreen. That night they left and drove one of the pool cars straight through to Normandy where their war adventures had really begun. Along the way, Midge told her friend that Bert was about to propose and Midge had frozen. She had not said yes or anything. She said she wanted to go to the Abbey at St. Michel and think, pray and then decide. The next day they went to the Abbey and after the tide subsided, they crossed the bridge to the island Abbey. After 345 steps to the top, they entered into the old cloisters area and found a functioning chapel and sat in the cool damp room in silence. Looking out the glassless windows of the chapel, the winter winds were blowing in adding to the discomfort. Her eyes began to tear. Maybe it was the wind or maybe it was something else. She reached into her handbag and pulled out a cloth wrapped object, unwrapped it and held a pouch in her hand. In it were two small moccasins and a feather. She held each in her hands for a few moments. She thought of the strong women in her life and the support each had given to her through the years. These keepsakes were not the end. They had helped her in some way make it this far in life but this was not the end but maybe just the beginning. Maybe she had come all the way to Europe just to find the right person to spend the rest of her life with. Maybe Bert was right, they were meant to meet and to be together. Finally, Midge leaned over the pew and hugged her friend and said, "Coreen, let!s go back to Fulda." Again Midge drove straight through. She talked all the way back, telling Coreen what the keepsakes had meant to her and why she had carried them with her all through France and into Germany.

The next day she showed up at Captain Waller!s office, knocked on the door and walked right past his staff sergeant into the commander!s office. Midge said "Yes, I would, as long as it was you." His face lit up and he asked formally "Will you Helen Elizabeth Schonebaum marry me Elbert Cecil Waller?" She jumped into his arms and said "Yes, I will!"

A week later Helen and Bert were married in Fulda witnessed by Coreen, Ester, Margaret and Marjorie. Several days later Martin and Ma received a telegram from Fulda, Germany. It was the first word that they had received from their daughter Helen since she told them she was staying in Germany for a while with the Red Cross to support the troops stationed there. The telegram was hand delivered to their house by Western Union and read:

Mr. and Mrs Schonebaum

Erskine Street Omaha, Neb

Met a great guy. Married him here in Fulda.

Will see you when I get home.

Mrs. Elbert C. Waller

THE END